HOMEWORK
Helpster™

Makes Homework Happen

learn faster
grade **3**
score higher

Have you forgotten a lesson?

Can't remember a math formula?

Do you need to double-check your facts?

Now it's simple and easy.

Just use the dividers to quickly find the answers you need.

Each page takes you to a different lesson on a different topic.

Each page summarizes lessons with examples and facts you need to

D1301068

How to use your
H O M E W O R K
Helpster™

Chapter

Lesson

Unique Design
Stands up! Stands out!
At home or on the go!

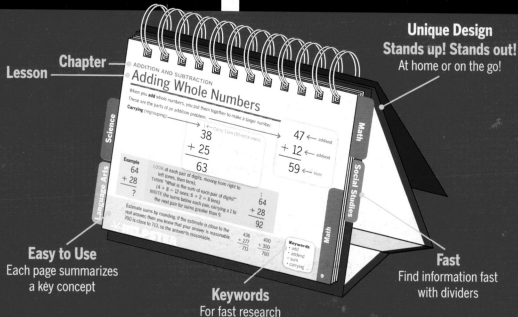

ADDITION AND SUBTRACTION
Adding Whole Numbers

When you **add** whole numbers, you put them together to make a larger number.

These are the parts of an addition problem:

Carrying (regrouping):

1 ← Carry 1 ten (10 extra ones).

$$38$$
$$+ 25$$
$$\overline{63}$$

$$47 \leftarrow \text{addend}$$
$$+ 12 \leftarrow \text{addend}$$
$$\overline{59} \leftarrow \text{sum}$$

Example

$$64$$
$$+ 28$$
$$\overline{?}$$

LOOK at each pair of digits, moving from right to
left (ones, then tens).
THINK "What is the sum of each pair of digits?"
$(4 + 8 = 12$ ones; $6 + 2 = 8$ tens)"
WRITE the sums below each pair, carrying a 1 to
the next pair for sums greater than 9.

$$1$$
$$64$$
$$+ 28$$
$$\overline{92}$$

Estimate sums by rounding. If the estimate is close to the
real answer, then you know that your answer is reasonable.
700 is close to 713, so the answer is reasonable.

$$436$$
$$+ 277$$
$$\overline{713}$$

$$400$$
$$+ 300$$
$$\overline{700}$$

Keywords
• add
• addend
• sum
• carrying

Easy to Use
Each page summarizes
a key concept

Keywords
For fast research

Fast
Find information fast
with dividers

Science

Language Arts

Math

Social Studies

Math

TimeLine™

TimeLine™
EXPLORERS
From Egypt to Mars

HISTORY UNFOLDS · More Brain Power

TimeLine™
INVENTIONS
From Rocks to Rockets

HISTORY UNFOLDS · More Brain Power

TimeLine™
PRESIDENTS
From Independence to Now

HISTORY UNFOLDS · More Brain Power

Vocabulary Power

200 words to know
for reading comprehension

Notes

Social Studies Contents

The Metric System

Scientists use the **metric system** to make measurements. In this system, mass is measured in **grams,** length is measured in **meters,** and volume is measured in **liters.**

In the metric system, all of the units are based on the number 10. A **prefix** in front of the unit name tells you how large or small something is.

Prefix name	Amount	Example
milli	$\frac{1}{1,000}$	A milliliter is $\frac{1}{1,000}$ of a liter.
centi	$\frac{1}{100}$	A centimeter is $\frac{1}{100}$ of a meter.
deci	$\frac{1}{10}$	A decigram is $\frac{1}{10}$ of a gram.
deka	10 times	A dekagram is 10 grams.
hecto	100 times	A hectoliter is 100 liters.
kilo	1,000 times	A kilometer is 1,000 meters.

This bottle holds 2 liters.

Keywords
- metric system
- grams
- meters
- liters
- prefix

Scientists prefer the metric system because it is easy to convert one type of measurement to another.

Social Studies Contents (continued)

SCIENTIFIC MEASUREMENT
Scientific Tools

When scientists collect data, they use many different tools to help them make observations and measurements. Three common tools are:

Microscopes: Used to observe things that are too small to see with the eye alone or even with a magnifier. With a microscope, biologists can see things such as individual animal cells, bacteria, and viruses.

Compasses: Used to find direction. A compass has a tiny magnet inside that is attracted to the earth's own magnetic poles. Geologists use compasses to find out which way structures in rocks are pointing.

Thermometers: Used to measure how hot and cold things are. Chemists use thermometers to measure the temperature of liquids and gases.

Tools allow scientists to extend their senses into ranges far beyond human and to levels beyond impressions such as "this looks small."

Keywords
- microscopes
- compasses
- thermometers

Social Studies **Keywords**

PHYSICAL SCIENCE
Force and Motion

When something moves, it's because a **force** is pushing or pulling on it. We encounter many different forces every day. Here are some of them.

▶ **Gravity** is a force that pulls things together. When you drop a ball, the earth's gravity pulls it down.

▶ **Friction** is a force that pushes against moving objects. The rougher the surface, the greater the friction. A hockey puck moves fast over ice because there is very little friction.

▶ **Magnetism** is a force that can either push or pull. Metals such as iron and steel are attracted to magnets.

A magnet doesn't touch a steel object to push or pull it. The magnet just has to get near the object.

Keywords
• force
• gravity
• friction
• magnetism

Social Studies **Keywords** (continued)

Energy

Science

Energy makes matter move and change. Like matter, energy comes in several different forms. It can be used right away or stored.

▶ **Light energy** is used by plants to grow.

▶ **Heat energy** is used to cook food.

▶ **Electrical energy** is used to power many different things.

▶ **Mechanical energy** is used to make things move.

▶ **Chemical energy** is stored in fuels and food.

▶ **Nuclear energy** is used in power plants and is what powers the sun.

Electrical

Chemical

Mechanical

Light

One of the most important laws of science is that energy can be changed from one form to another, but it can never be created or destroyed.

Keywords
• energy
• electrical
• mechanical
• chemical
• nuclear

Communities and Culture

Communities are places and people. A town or city where people live is a community. A group of people who share a culture can also be a community.

Culture is the word for the beliefs and way of life shared by a group of people: how they live and work, their faith, their language, their way of dressing, their art.

Sometimes everyone in a community shares the same culture. In the United States, people of different cultures live together in communities. Large cities such as Los Angeles, California, and Houston, Texas, are communities. So are small towns such as Crowley, Louisiana, and Middlebury, Vermont.

Cultural communities such as the Moslem community or the Mexican-American community are made up of people who live in different places but who share a common culture.

The word *community* comes from the Latin word for "common."
People in a community have things and places in common.

Keywords
- community
- culture

Social Studies

✳HELPSTER

PHYSICAL SCIENCE
Matter

Matter is all the material that makes up the universe.
All matter is made of tiny particles called **atoms.**
Matter has three common **states,** or forms.

▶ **Solids** have a definite shape and structure. In
  solids, the atoms are packed close together and
  move very little.

▶ **Liquids** have no definite shape. They change their
  shape to fit the container they are in. The atoms of
  liquids are more spread out and vibrate faster then
  those in solids.

▶ **Gases** have no definite shape or size. Atoms in
  gases are very spread out and move very quickly.

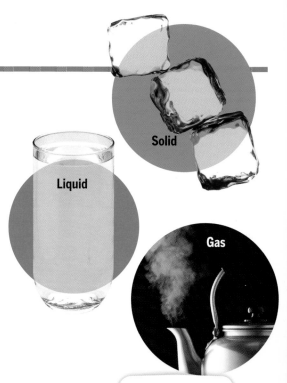

Solid

Liquid

Gas

Plasma is a fourth state of matter. It's like a superheated
gas that glows. The sun is mostly plasma.

Keywords
- matter
- atoms
- states
- solids
- liquids
- gases
- plasma

Learning About Your Community

There's a lot to find out in order to know your community! You need to learn about the place and the people. And you need to find out about your community's past to understand how it got the way it is today. Here are some questions to get started.

THE PLACE	THE PEOPLE	THE HISTORY
▶ Look at a map of your community. Then see if you can find your community on a U.S. map.	▶ How many people live in your community?	▶ Who were the first people to live where your community is now?
▶ Do you live in a **city** (a large community), a **suburb** (a smaller community close to a city), or a **town** (a small community)?	▶ What kinds of work do people do? What kinds of businesses are there?	▶ How and when did your community get its name?
▶ Is your community **urban** (a city) or **rural** (in the country)?		

Keywords
- city
- suburb
- town
- urban
- rural

Looking for answers? Contact your community's chamber of commerce, or visit your local library.

✳HELPSTER

2

EARTH SCIENCE
The Stars

Even though the stars we see at night look like little dots, they are actually large spheres of hot glowing gas, just like the sun.

Many of the stars we see are actually bigger than the sun, but because they are so far away, they look tiny. The sun is the only star in our solar system. The other stars make up our **galaxy,** which is called the **Milky Way.**

At night, stars appear to make shapes in the sky, called **constellations.** The constellations appear to move because the earth is rotating.

Astronomers estimate that the Milky Way galaxy includes more than 200 billion stars.

Keywords
- galaxy
- Milky Way
- constellations

✳HELPSTER

35

Living Together

By living together in a community, people can help one another. They can work together to solve problems.

▶ The people who live in a community are its **citizens**.

▶ Each community is managed by a **local government**, the people who run the city.

▶ In America, people who can vote **elect** most members of the local government.

▶ In most communities the leader of the local government is the **mayor**.

▶ Local governments make rules, or **laws**, to keep people safe and to help the government work.

Social Studies

The 2000 U.S. census listed around 20,000 cities, towns, and villages with their own separate governments in the United States.

Keywords
- citizens
- local government
- elect
- mayor
- laws

✳HELPSTER

3

EARTH SCIENCE
The Moon

The moon is about one-quarter the size of Earth. It is our only natural **satellite.** It orbits Earth once every 27 $\frac{1}{3}$ days, going through a cycle of **phases.**

Phases happen because the moon reflects light from the sun. Half of the moon is always lit, but here on Earth, we don't always see the lit side. When we see half the lit side and half the dark side, the moon is in a **quarter** phase. When we see just a tiny sliver of the lit side, it's a **crescent.** The only time we see the entire lit side is during a **full moon.**

During a **new moon,** we can't see the moon at all because its dark side is facing Earth.

Keywords
- satellite
- phases
- quarter
- crescent
- full moon
- new moon

Working Together

In any community, people work at many different jobs.

Working in the Community

Jobs provide **goods** and **services** for people. *Goods* are things that people buy or sell—anything from a pair of jeans to a house. *Services* are the jobs that people do to help others. People who work in banks, restaurants, and as police officers all provide services.

People work to supply their needs and wants. *Needs* are the things they must have for survival: food, clothing, and shelter. *Wants* are the things that people would like to have but do not need for survival, such as a DVD or a skateboard.

Consumers are people who buy goods and services. Communities have many different businesses where consumers shop.

Social Studies

When you shop at a store, you buy goods, use a service, and supply your needs and wants. You are being a consumer at a business.

Keywords
- goods
- services
- consumers

4

EARTH SCIENCE
The Sun

The sun is the only star in our solar system. A star is a ball of hot glowing gas. The sun's gravity holds the earth and other planets in **orbit** around it.

Earth gets all its light and most of its heat from the sun. One side of Earth is always lit by the sun. That is daytime. The dark side is night. Every day Earth completes one full **rotation,** or spin, on its **axis.** As it does, daylight moves across the planet.

Earth orbits the sun once each year. Because Earth's axis is tilted, different parts of the planet are lit more or less by the sun at different times of the year. This is why we have seasons.

Keywords
- orbit
- rotation
- axis

33

The Shape of the Land

A community's location affects much about its physical appearance and its ways of life.
Landforms (the shape of the land) are a key part of location. Major landforms are shown here.

1 **Hill** rise of higher land

2 **Mountain** large mass of land rising high above surrounding land

3 **Mountain Range** row of mountains

4 **Valley** low land lying between mountains or hills

5 **Plateau** area of high, usually flat land

6 **Plain** area of low land, mostly flat or slightly rolling

7 **Coast** land at the edge of an ocean or sea

8 **Peninsula** extension of land mostly surrounded by water

9 **Canyon** narrow valley with steep sides

10 **Island** land completely surrounded by water

Mountain

Canyon

Coast

Island

Social Studies

Geography is the study of all of Earth's features, including physical
features such as land and water and human-made features such as
cities or dams.

Keywords
- landforms
- hill
- mountain
- valley
- plateau
- plain
- coast
- peninsula
- canyon
- island

5

EARTH SCIENCE
The Solar System

The solar system is our neighborhood in space. It is made up of one **star** (the sun), eight **planets,** and more than 100 **moons.**

The sun is the center of the solar system. All the planets **orbit**, or go around, the sun. Moons orbit planets. All the planets except Mercury and Venus have moons. The following chart gives data for each planet.

Name	Diameter (kilometers)	Distance from Sun (kilometers)*	What's It Made of?
Mercury	4,879	57,909,175	Rock
Venus	12,104	108,208,930	Rock
Earth	12,756	149,597,890	Rock
Mars	6,787	227,936,640	Rock
Jupiter	142,800	778,412,020	Gas
Saturn	120,660	1,426,725,400	Gas
Uranus	51,118	2,870,972,200	Gas
Neptune	49,528	4,498,252,900	Gas

Source: NASA

*Distances from the sun vary during the planets' orbits.

Recently, scientists have discovered several new objects orbiting the sun beyond the dwarf planet Pluto, but they are not sure if they are true planets.

Keywords
- star
- planets
- moons
- orbit

✳HELPSTER

Bodies of Water

Before modern transportation changed travel, many communities began along coasts or by rivers. Major types of **bodies of water** are shown here.

1 Bay part of an ocean or lake that is partially enclosed by land (smaller than a gulf)

2 Channel passage between two bodies of water or through shallow water

3 Gulf large area of an ocean that is partially enclosed by land (larger than a bay)

4 Lake body of water completely surrounded by land

5 Ocean the body of water covering about three-quarters of Earth's surface, divided into Atlantic, Pacific, Indian, and Arctic oceans. (Some sources also include the Southern Ocean, which is the new name for the ocean surrounding Antarctica.)

6 River large stream of moving water that empties into another river, a lake, or the ocean

Social Studies

Sea can be another name for the ocean. Sea also can mean a large body of salt water mostly enclosed by land, such as the Black Sea.

Keywords
- bodies of water
- bay
- channel
- gulf
- lake
- ocean
- river
- sea

HELPSTER

6

EARTH SCIENCE
Weather

The word **weather** describes the conditions in the air at a given place and time. A weather forecast predicts what the weather will be by measuring the following conditions:

▶ **Temperature:** how hot or cold the air is (measured with a **thermometer**).

▶ **Pressure:** whether the air pressure is rising or falling (measured with a **barometer**). High pressure usually means fair weather; low pressure usually means a storm is likely.

▶ **Wind Speed**: how fast the wind is blowing (measured with an **anemometer**).

▶ **Wind Direction**: what direction the wind is blowing (measured with a wind vane).

▶ **Humidity:** how much water vapor is in the air.

▶ **Cloud Cover:** how much sunlight to expect.

▶ **Precipitation:** the amount of rain, freezing rain, snow, sleet, or hail.

Thermometer

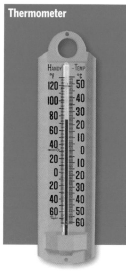

Barometer

Keywords
• weather
• thermometer
• barometer
• anemometer
• humidity
• precipitation
• climate

While weather describes the current conditions, **climate** tells the average weather conditions in an area over a long period of time.

✳HELPSTER

Seeing Earth on a Globe

A **globe** is a model of Earth. Round like Earth, a globe shows land and bodies of water in their true shapes.

▶ The North Pole is the farthest north spot on Earth.

▶ The South Pole is the farthest south spot on Earth.

▶ The **equator** is an imaginary line around Earth. It divides a globe in half between the North and South poles.

▶ The Northern **Hemisphere** is the half of Earth between the equator and the North Pole.

▶ The Southern Hemisphere is the half of Earth between the equator and the South Pole.

▶ An imaginary line between the poles divides Earth into the Eastern Hemisphere and the Western Hemisphere.

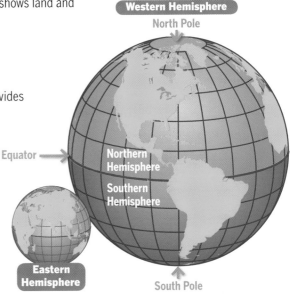

Western Hemisphere
North Pole
Equator →
Northern Hemisphere
Southern Hemisphere
Eastern Hemisphere
South Pole

Social Studies

A hemisphere is half of a sphere or ball. *Hemi* is the Greek word for "half."

Keywords
• globe
• equator
• hemisphere

✳ HELPSTER

7

EARTH SCIENCE
Pollution

Pollution happens when the water, air, or land is **contaminated** with harmful materials. While some pollution is caused naturally, most is caused by humans:

▶ **Water Pollution:** When chemicals from factories or waste water from sewers get into rivers, lakes, and streams, they not only harm animals living in them but also make the water undrinkable.

▶ **Air Pollution:** When smoke from factories and cars gets into the air, it makes the air unhealthy to breathe and causes other problems, including **acid rain**.

▶ **Land Pollution:** When trash and litter are dumped on the ground, it not only looks bad but also can contaminate drinking water.

You can help reduce pollution by picking up litter and not dumping poisonous chemicals down sink drains.

Keywords
• pollution
• contaminated
• acid rain

✳HELPSTER

Seeing Earth on a Map

A **map** is a picture of a place. Maps are more convenient to carry than globes to show locations on Earth. Like a globe, a map can show all of Earth. Maps also can focus on very small places.

Map title—tells what the map is about

Map symbols—stand for real places or things on Earth

Map **key** or legend—tells the meaning of the map symbols

Distance scale—compares distance on the map to distance on Earth

Compass rose—shows directions on the map

Grid lines—divide a map into sections to make it easier to locate something

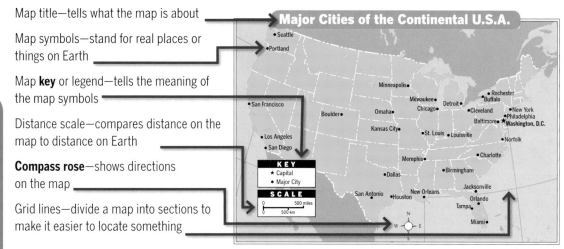

Major Cities of the Continental U.S.A.

KEY
★ Capital
• Major City

SCALE
0   500 miles
0   500 km

Seattle, Portland, Minneapolis, San Francisco, Milwaukee, Detroit, Rochester, Buffalo, Chicago, Cleveland, New York, Boulder, Omaha, Baltimore, Washington, D.C., Philadelphia, Los Angeles, Kansas City, St. Louis, Louisville, San Diego, Norfolk, Memphis, Charlotte, Dallas, Birmingham, San Antonio, New Orleans, Houston, Jacksonville, Orlando, Tampa, Miami

Social Studies

Cardinal directions are north, south, east, and west. Intermediate directions are northeast, southeast, northwest, and southwest.

Keywords
• map
• key
• compass rose

✳HELPSTER

8

EARTH SCIENCE
Natural Resources

Science

A **natural resource** is something that we get from the environment that we depend on to help us live. Resources come in three different forms.

▶ Renewable resources can be used and replaced. They include soil and products from plants and animals, including food.

▶ Nonrenewable resources are things such as oil, coal, and natural gas that have a limited supply and will eventually run out.

▶ Inexhaustible resources are resources that will never run out. They include sunlight, air, and water. However, air and water are only inexhaustible if we keep them clean!

Renewable
(apples)

Nonrenewable
(coal)

Inexhaustible
(solar energy)

Recycling means putting materials such as metal and paper through a process so they can be used again. This helps conserve resources and reduce waste.

Keywords
- natural resource
- renewable resources
- nonrenewable resources
- inexhaustible resourses
- recycling

The United States: The Land

Physical maps show the shapes of the land and water in a place. They can indicate what grows where, what the land is used for, or the climate. This physical map focuses on **landforms** in the United States.

Landform Map of the Continental U.S.A.

Social Studies

The highest place in the United States is Mt. McKinley in Alaska.
The lowest place is in Death Valley in California.

Keywords
• physical maps
• landforms

HELPSTER

9

EARTH SCIENCE
Glaciers

Glaciers are slow-moving masses of ice that flow across the earth's surface, moving rocks and shaping the land. There are three main types of glaciers.

▶ **Valley glaciers** form in mountains. Snow collects on top of the mountain and slowly turns to ice. Like a river, valley glaciers move downhill as new snow falling at the top of the glacier pushes the ice forward.

▶ **Piedmont glaciers** form at the base of mountains where valley glaciers join together.

▶ **Ice caps** are continent-sized glaciers that form near the earth's poles. They store most of the earth's freshwater.

Ice cap

Piedmont glacier

Because of global warming, glaciers and ice caps are melting, and the extra water is causing the sea level to rise.

Keywords
- glaciers
- valley glaciers
- piedmont glaciers
- ice caps

✳️HELPSTER

GEOGRAPHY
The 50 States

Political maps show nations, states, and cities. This political map features the 50 states of the United States. It also shows the borders between the United States, Canada, and Mexico.

Because Alaska and Hawaii are not part of the continental United States, maps often show them in separate boxes, called **insets**.

Keywords
- political maps
- insets

Earthquakes

Science

When earthquakes happen, the surface of the earth suddenly starts shaking, often causing damage to buildings and injuring people.

Earthquakes take place because the outer layer, or **crust,** of the earth is not solid. Instead it is made up of many individual pieces called **plates.** Plates are separated by large cracks called **faults.** When two plates move past each other at a fault, an earthquake happens.

Scientists can measure earthquakes and their **aftershocks** (smaller movements after the main earthquake). They use an instrument called a **seismograph,** which measures and records the energy of the earthquake's vibrations.

When earthquakes take place under the ocean, they create large destructive waves called **tsunamis.**

Keywords
- crust
- plates
- faults
- aftershocks
- seismograph
- tsunamis

27

Reading a World Map

World maps show the 7 continents, 4 oceans, and almost 200 countries on Earth.

Mapmakers use imaginary lines of **latitude** and **longitude** to locate places on Earth. Distance between the lines is measured in degrees (°). Latitude lines run east and west around the globe. Distance is measured in degrees north and south of the equator. Longitude lines run north and south between the poles. Distance is measured in degrees east and west of the longitude line called the prime meridian.

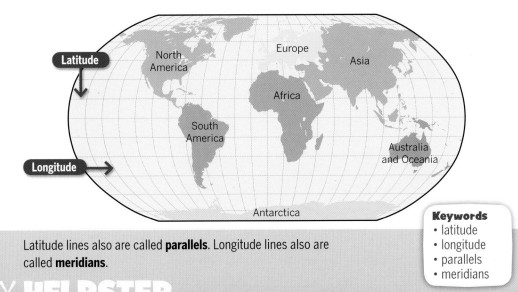

Latitude lines also are called **parallels**. Longitude lines also are called **meridians**.

Keywords
- latitude
- longitude
- parallels
- meridians

Social Studies

✳HELPSTER

EARTH SCIENCE
Soil

Soil is made up of minerals from broken-down rocks as well as **humus,** matter composed of dead plants and animals that have decayed. Different soils have different properties.

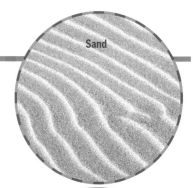
Sand

Soil Name	Grain Size	Texture	Reaction to Water
Clay	Microscopic	Sticky	Drains very slowly
Silt	Fine (like flour)	Soft	Drains slowly
Sand	Coarse (like sugar)	Rough	Drains fast
Loam	Mixture of all three	Varies	Drains easily but holds water for plants

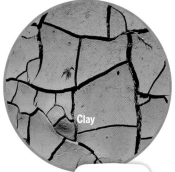
Clay

Keywords
- humus
- clay
- silt
- sand
- loam

Loam soils are usually the best for growing plants, because they almost never get too wet or too dry.

✳️HELPSTER

People and the Earth

Geography is about places but it also describes how people interact with Earth.

- ▶ People change Earth by adding human features such as cities and roads.

- ▶ People use Earth's **natural resources** such as water, trees, and minerals.

- ▶ People adapt to conditions such as climate.

- ▶ People can cause **pollution** and also can work to prevent or change it.

Social Studies

Environment can mean all of the human and physical features of a place. Sometimes, however, people use the word to mean only the natural world: land, water, and air.

Keywords
- natural resources
- pollution
- environment

12

✳ HELPSTER

EARTH SCIENCE
Weathering

Weathering is the breaking down of rocks and minerals by forces of nature. There are two main types of weathering.

▶ **Chemical weathering** happens when water and natural acids react with the minerals in rock and cause them to dissolve. It usually happens in areas where there is a great deal of rain.

▶ **Physical weathering** happens when rocks are broken by forces such as ice, wind, and running water. When water seeps into cracks in rocks and freezes, it expands, causing the rock to split.

Chemical weathering

Physical weathering

Sometimes, chemical and physical weathering go hand in hand. For example, plants growing in the cracks of rocks can cause both physical and chemical weathering.

Keywords
• chemical weathering
• physical weathering

✳HELPSTER

25

Coming to America

Who were the first people in the Americas? Historians believe that humans first arrived here thousands of years ago from Asia.

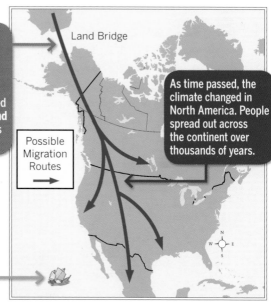

Thousands of years ago, glaciers covered much of Earth's surface. Solid land connected Asia and North America. Historians believe that hunting families followed large animals across this **land bridge**. (Today, water divides the two continents.)

Land Bridge

As time passed, the climate changed in North America. People spread out across the continent over thousands of years.

Possible Migration Routes →

Some historians believe that ancient peoples also traveled from Asia by sea and reached South America.

Social Studies

When historians and other scholars find an **artifact**—an object made by humans—they use scientific methods to date it. This helps explain what may have happened in ancient times.

Keywords
• land bridge
• artifact

✳HELPSTER

13

Rocks

Earth is a planet made of rock. **Geologists,** scientists who study the earth, have found that rocks form in three different ways:

Igneous rocks form from hot melted rock. When the liquid rock cools, solid minerals form. Igneous rocks can form either below the surface or above the earth's crust.

Metamorphic rocks are rocks whose minerals changed because of heat and pressure. Most metamorphic rocks form deep below the surface of the earth.

Sedimentary rocks are made from pieces of other rocks that have been joined together.

Minerals are the building blocks of rocks. There are more than 2,000 different minerals.

Keywords
- geologists
- igneous
- metamorphic
- sedimentary
- minerals

24

Many People, Many Cultures

As the first Americans spread out across the continent, they developed a wide variety of cultures, or ways of life. People living in one area often shared a similar culture.

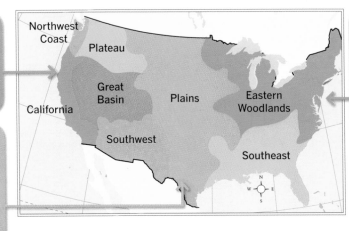

Climate shaped cultures. The peoples of California lived in a gentle climate where they could find all of the food that they needed.

Contact shaped cultures. When the peoples of the Plains came in contact with Europeans, they learned about horses. In time, horses became central to their lives.

Resources shaped cultures. Forests surrounded the peoples of the Eastern Woodlands, so wood played an important part in their lives.

Northwest Coast

Plateau

Great Basin

Plains

Eastern Woodlands

California

Southwest

Southeast

Native means "born in or originating in." Native Americans—also known as **American Indians**—are descendants of the first humans who lived here.

Keywords
- climate
- resources
- American Indians

HELPSTER

14

LIFE SCIENCE
Avoiding Diseases

A **disease** is something that makes you sick. Many diseases can be avoided by following some simple rules and living wisely.

▶ **Practice Good Hygiene:** Many diseases are spread by **germs.** By washing your hands and covering your mouth when you sneeze and cough, you can stop germs from spreading.

▶ **Exercise:** Exercise keeps you strong and helps defend your body against germs.

▶ **Avoid Eating Sugar and Fats:** Too many sugary and fatty foods can make you overweight, which can lead to diseases such as diabetes and high blood pressure.

▶ **Avoid the Sun:** Too much sun can cause skin cancer. Cover up or wear sunblock when you are outside.

▶ **Avoid Alcohol and Tobacco:** Using these can cause many diseases of the lungs, heart, liver, and throat.

Keywords
- disease
- hygiene
- germs

Peoples of the East Coast

Native Americans living between the Atlantic Ocean and the Mississippi River shared many beliefs and practices. Their culture is called the **Eastern Woodlands** culture.

EASTERN WOODLANDS

▶ Thick forests covered the eastern half of North America. The peoples who lived in them made cooking vessels, tools, and art from wood.

▶ Some peoples were farmers who cleared the land to raise food. Some peoples hunted for forest animals such as deer, bears, and birds.

▶ In the Northeast, many homes were made of wood and bark. In the Southeast, homes often had straw roofs.

▶ The peoples of the Southeast were among the most advanced north of Mexico.

Some Eastern Woodlands Peoples

Algonquians
Delaware
Mohawk
Powhatan
Tuscarora
Cherokee
Creek

Native American longhouses on Manhattan Island

The Granger Collection, New York

Social Studies

A group of Native Americans who share a language and customs is sometimes called a **tribe**. While the Eastern Woodlands region was home to different tribes (*see* box), they had many ways of life in common.

Keywords
• Native Americans
• Eastern Woodlands
• tribe

✳HELPSTER

15

LIFE SCIENCE
Fitness

A big part of staying healthy is exercising to maintain your **physical fitness.**
Fitness has three main parts.

Flexibility is how much movement you have in your joints and how far your muscles can stretch.

Muscle strength is how much weight you can move, and muscle **endurance** means how long you can keep going before your muscles get tired.

Heart and lung endurance is measured by how hard you breathe and how fast your heart beats when you do exercise. It's also measured by how fast it takes for your breathing to get back to normal when you stop exercising.

Staying physically fit helps your body systems work more efficiently, so you have more energy.

Keywords
- physical fitness
- flexibility
- strength
- endurance

22

Peoples of the Plains, Plateau, and Great Basin

Some Plains, Plateau, and Great Basin Peoples
Mandan
Sioux
Cheyenne
Comanche
Nez Percé
Shoshones
Ute

Geography greatly influenced the cultures of the Plains, Plateau, and Great Basin peoples.

PLAINS
▶ Buffalo provided food, shelter, and clothing for most of the Plains peoples.

PLATEAU
▶ Between the Rocky and Cascade mountains, the Plateau peoples were in a crossroads through which many tribes passed. In the harsh winters, they lived in log houses built partly underground.

GREAT BASIN
▶ The western desert called the Great Basin is incredibly hot and dry, a very difficult place to survive. For the American Indians who lived there, life was a constant search for food and water.

Buffalo hunt

The Granger Collection, New York

People who move from place to place, usually in search of food and water, are called **nomads**. Many Plains tribes were nomadic. They carried all of their possessions on horseback as they followed the buffalo.

Social Studies

Keyword
• nomads

✳HELPSTER

16

LIFE SCIENCE
Eating for Health

Scientists have classified all the food we eat into different **food groups.**
Balancing your diet by eating the correct amount from each group
every day can help you stay healthy.

▶ **Grains** (includes bread and cereal) provide energy but are high in **starch.**

▶ **Vegetables** provide vitamins and minerals.

▶ **Fruits** also provide vitamins and minerals.

▶ **Oils** provide essential fatty acids that are necessary to stay
healthy. Most of us get enough oil when we eat nuts,
fish, cooking oil, and salad dressing.

▶ **Milk** and other dairy products provide **protein**
and calcium, but many foods in this group are high in fat.

▶ **Meat and beans** provide protein and iron. Lean and
low-fat meats and poultry are best. Fish, eggs, nuts,
and seeds are also part of this group.

| Grains | Vegetables | Fruits | Oils | Milk | Meat and beans |

Eating too many foods high in sugar, starch, and fat can
lead to diseases like diabetes later in life. But taking part
in physical activity can fight the effects of these foods.

Keywords
- food groups
- starch
- protein

21

Peoples of the Southwest

The Native American cultures of the Southwest focused on survival in a dry land.

SOUTHWEST

▶ The Anasazi culture was one of the oldest in North America. It began more than 2,000 years ago in what is now the Four Corners region of the United States, where Colorado, Utah, Arizona, and New Mexico meet.

▶ Like the Anasazi, many later Southwest peoples built homes out of **adobe**, bricks made of clay and straw. Others, like the Navajo, built homes of wood and earth.

▶ Peoples of the Southwest farmed corn, beans, squash, and other crops. Some were great sheepherders.

Some Southwest Peoples
Hopi
Zuni
Navajo
Apache

Ancient cliff dwellings in Mesa Verde National Park, Colorado

The typical adobe building had so many rooms that the Spanish explorers called this type of home a **pueblo**, their word for "town" or "village." Over time, the people who lived in them were called the Pueblo peoples.

Keywords
• adobe
• pueblo

Social Studies

✳HELPSTER

17

LIFE SCIENCE
Human Development

From the time we are born, our bodies go through many changes as we grow older. These changes are marked by the following stages of **development**.

Baby 0 to 1 year old	Toddler 1 to 3 years old	Child 3 to 11 years old	Adolescent 11 to 18 years old	Adult 19 to 65 years old	Elderly 65 and above
Babies need constant care and cannot even feed themselves. Their bodies grow fast, with many changes.	Toddlers begin to move by themselves, eat, and speak. Their bodies grow fast but with fewer changes.	Children can walk, talk, play, and care for themselves. While their bodies are still growing, the changes are much slower.	Body changes happen as young adults become physically mature. They reach adult height and weight.	Growth is slow, and different body systems begin to break down.	Growth stops, and **aging** is more rapid. Many body systems begin to fail.

Keywords
- development
- aging

20

Peoples of the West Coast

Along the northwest Pacific coast and in California, **American Indians** lived rich lives focused on the sea.

NORTHWEST COAST

▶ Northwest Coast peoples lived on the strip of land between the ocean and the mountains. The climate was wet and cool.

▶ Surrounded by forests, they used wood in many ways, including for **totem poles**, carved and painted posts that tell a family's history.

▶ Great traders, they traveled on rivers and the sea in giant canoes.

CALIFORNIA

▶ A mild climate made it possible for the California peoples to find all of the food that they needed.

▶ They were highly skilled basket makers, using grasses, barks, reeds, and roots.

Some West Coast Peoples

Haida
Makah
Pomo
Yokuts
Chumash

Kadjuk bird pole,
Ketchikan, Alaska

Social Studies

People who can find their food by hunting wild animals and gathering wild food are called **hunter-gatherers**.

Keywords
• American Indians
• totem poles
• hunter-gatherers

HELPSTER

18

LIFE SCIENCE
Endangered Animals

A species is **endangered** when its population becomes so small that the members have a hard time reproducing. Here are the main reasons this happens:

▶ **Habitat Destruction:** When people build homes, factories, and roads, they often destroy animal **habitats**. As more habitats are destroyed, there are fewer places animals and plants can live, so their populations decrease.

▶ **Hunting and Trapping:** Some animals, such as whales and elephants, have been hunted so much that there are very few of them left.

If care is taken by humans now and in the future, the dwindling populations of endangered animals can grow.

Bengal tiger

African elephant

Humpback whale

The cutting down of trees in tropical rain forests has caused many species of animals to become endangered and extinct.

Keywords
• endangered
• habitats

Peoples of Mesoamerica

Native Americans in Mesoamerica—present-day Mexico and Central America—built great cities.

- ▶ The **Mayas** built around 100 cities in the jungle. Each had its own government and powerful religious leaders.

- ▶ The **Aztecs** lived in what is now Mexico. They controlled a large empire of millions of people.

- ▶ The Mayas and the Aztecs traded foods such as corn and fish, as well as cloth and other products, in great central markets.

GULF OF MEXICO

Tenochtitlán

Aztec Civilization

Maya Civilization

PACIFIC OCEAN

Social Studies

The Aztec capital city was Tenochtitlán. After it was destroyed, modern-day Mexico City was built on the same site.

Keywords
- Mayas
- Aztecs

HELPSTER

19

LIFE SCIENCE
Extinct Animals

Over the years, many animals have become **extinct,** which means that all the members of the **species** have died out. Animals become extinct for two main reasons:

▶ Extinction usually happens when environmental conditions change faster than a species can **adapt** to them. These changes can happen slowly, as when the climate changes over time, or they can happen quickly, as when a volcano erupts.

▶ Sometimes, all the members of a species are killed off by other animals. In modern times, humans have made many species extinct.

Fossils preserved in rocks give scientists clues about animals that have become extinct.

Some scientists believe that sudden climate changes caused by a huge asteroid crashing into Earth led to the dinosaurs becoming extinct.

Keywords
- extinct
- species
- adapt
- fossils

Settling America

More than 500 years ago, Europeans came to the Americas and began to settle here. They claimed land for their rulers.

▶ **Christopher Columbus** sailed across the Atlantic, looking for a short route to Asia. When he reached the Americas in 1492, he claimed the land for Spain.

▶ Other explorers for Spain followed. They claimed land in what is now Florida, Mexico, and the southwestern United States.

▶ France claimed land in what is now Canada and the central United States.

▶ England claimed and settled on land along the Atlantic coast of what is now the United States and Canada.

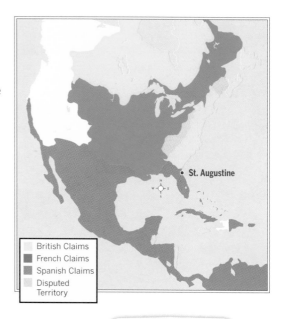

St. Augustine

British Claims
French Claims
Spanish Claims
Disputed Territory

Social Studies

St. Augustine, founded by the Spanish in 1565, was the first permanent **European settlement** in what is now the United States.

Keywords
• Christopher Columbus
• St. Augustine
• European settlement

✳HELPSTER

20

LIFE SCIENCE
Insects

Even though scientists have discovered more than 750,000 different types of insects, all members of this animal group have the following things in common:

▶ All insects have three main body parts: a head, an **abdomen,** and a **thorax.**

▶ True insects have six legs and many also have wings.

▶ Instead of having a skeleton inside their bodies, insects have a hard outer skeleton—an **exoskeleton**—which they shed as they grow.

▶ Insects are **invertebrates;** they have no backbone.

▶ All insects lay eggs and many go through **metamorphosis** during their life cycle.

Head

Thorax

Abdomen

Many insects, including ants and bees, live in large groups called **colonies.**

Keywords
• abdomen
• thorax
• exoskeleton
• invertebrates
• metamorphosis
• colonies

Colonial Communities

Europeans created **colonies** in America—settlements ruled by a different country. The 13 British colonies would later become the United States.

▶ English settlers founded **Jamestown** in Virginia in 1607. It was the first permanent English settlement in what would become the United States.

▶ **Plymouth** and Boston were the first settlements in Massachusetts. Boston became one of the largest colonial cities.

▶ Philadelphia in Pennsylvania was another large and important colonial city.

▶ Charleston was the first community in the Carolinas. Soon it was one of the wealthiest cities in the colonies.

▶ Spanish settlers founded Santa Fe in what is now New Mexico.

Tercentenary Monument, Jamestown, Virginia

American Indians had lived where the colonies developed. They were pushed farther west as more Europeans claimed their land.

Keywords
- colonies
- Jamestown
- Plymouth

Social Studies

✳HELPSTER

21

LIFE SCIENCE
Fish

Fish have special adaptations that allow them to live in the water. While they come in many shapes and sizes, fish have the following things in common:

▶ Fish have **scales** covering their bodies, which help them glide through the water.

▶ Fish lay eggs. Some fish, including sharks, hold the eggs inside their bodies until they hatch. This makes it look like they are giving birth to live babies.

▶ Fish are **cold-blooded,** which means that their body temperature changes with the environment.

▶ Fish breathe by using **gills.** These special structures take the oxygen out of the water.

Salmon

Silky shark

The skeletons of sharks are made from **cartilage** instead of bone. Cartilage is a tough, elastic connective tissue. Humans have it in their joints, nose, and outer ear.

Keywords
• fish
• scales
• cold-blooded
• gills
• cartilage

16

The Declaration of Independence

Over time, those living in the British colonies began to feel that Great Britain's treatment of them was unfair. Finally, in 1776, the colonists declared their independence.

▶ In 1775, Americans clashed with the British at Lexington and Concord in Massachusetts. This was the beginning of the **American Revolution**.

▶ On July 4, 1776, colonial leaders signed the **Declaration of Independence**.

▶ **Thomas Jefferson** and others wrote the Declaration. It told why the colonists were angry with Britain. It explained that the colonists wanted a new government, independent from Britain.

▶ The Declaration stated that everyone is "created equal."

▶ The 13 colonies became 13 united states.

In 1770, six years before the signing of the Declaration of Independence, there were probably more than 2 million Europeans and Africans living in the British colonies in North America.

Keywords
- American Revolution
- Declaration of Independence
- Thomas Jefferson

Social Studies

✳HELPSTER

LIFE SCIENCE
Amphibians

Many **amphibians** have special body structures that allow them to live both on land and in the water. Amphibians have the following things in common:

Rough-skin newt

▶ While they don't have scales, amphibians have rough skin that must stay moist.

▶ Female amphibians lay soft eggs in water, where they are fertilized by males.

▶ Amphibians are **cold-blooded,** changing their body temperature to meet their surroundings.

▶ Amphibians have backbones, and most have lungs.

▶ Some amphibians can breathe through their skin.

Green tree frog

▶ Some amphibians, including frogs, go through **metamorphosis.**

Many amphibians start their lives in the water and then live on the land as adults.

Keywords
• amphibians
• cold-blooded
• metamorphosis

✳HELPSTER

15

The Constitution of the United States

The new nation needed a plan for its government, or **constitution**. In 1787, citizens from all 13 states met in Philadelphia to create the U.S. Constitution. It is still used today.

▶ The Constitution is a plan for the U.S. national, or **federal**, government. States and cities have their own governments.

▶ The Constitution set up a **democracy**. This means that the people of the nation hold the power to rule. Citizens who can vote choose representatives to run the government.

▶ We can change the Constitution by voting for additions called **amendments**.

▶ The first 10 amendments to the Constitution are called the **Bill of Rights**.

Social Studies

The National Archives in Washington, D.C., has one of the original copies of the U.S. Constitution.

Keywords
- constitution
- federal
- democracy
- amendments
- Bill of Rights

LIFE SCIENCE
Reptiles

Reptiles are a large group of animals with many different body shapes. Despite their differences, reptiles have the following things in common:

▶ Most reptiles live on land, but some spend part of the time in water.

▶ Reptiles are **cold-blooded,** and they have **scales** to protect their strong, waterproof skin. Some reptiles, like turtles, also have shells or large plates for protection. Though some people think reptiles' skin is slimy, it's actually dry.

▶ Most reptiles lay eggs that have a thick, leathery shell to protect the developing offspring from drying out inside.

▶ Reptiles have backbones and use their lungs to breathe air.

Collared lizard

Desert tortoise

Most scientists believe that dinosaurs are an extinct part of the reptile family.

Keywords
• reptiles
• cold-blooded
• scales

14

The U.S. Government

A government makes and enforces the rules to manage a city, state, or nation. In the United States, these three levels of government share some powers. They also have separate powers.

The federal, or national, government has three branches, or parts. The Constitution balances powers among the three branches. Each branch makes sure that the others do their jobs according to the Constitution.

Federal Government

Executive Branch
The president
makes sure laws are obeyed.

Legislative Branch
Congress
makes laws.

Judicial Branch
The Supreme Court
makes sure that laws follow
the Constitution.

Social Studies

LIFE SCIENCE
Birds

Birds can be found living in a wide range of environments, from steamy tropical rain forests to cold and windy Antarctica. All birds have the following things in common:

▶ Even though some birds, such as penguins and ostriches, can't fly, all birds have wings.

▶ Most birds have a good sense of hearing but a poor sense of smell.

▶ All birds lay hard-shelled eggs when they reproduce.

▶ Birds have beaks, but they do not have teeth.

▶ Birds have **feathers** covering their bodies and **scales** on their feet.

▶ Birds are **warm-blooded** and have a backbone.

▶ Birds use their lungs to breathe air.

Different birds have differently shaped beaks, depending on the types of food they eat.

Ostrich

Adélie penguin

American bald eagle

Keywords
- birds
- feathers
- scales
- warm-blooded

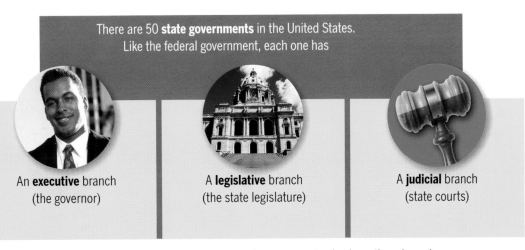

There are 50 **state governments** in the United States.
Like the federal government, each one has

An **executive** branch
(the governor)

A **legislative** branch
(the state legislature)

A **judicial** branch
(state courts)

Local governments manage cities and towns. Many local governments also have three branches. The city council makes laws. A mayor or city manager makes sure the laws are obeyed. And local courts deal with people who do not follow the laws.

Social Studies

Counties are another form of local government. The first counties were set up in the Virginia colony in the 1600s. Today, counties often oversee services that are shared by several cities or towns.

Keywords
- executive branch
- legislative branch
- judicial branch
- state governments
- local governments
- counties

LIFE SCIENCE
Mammals

Humans belong to a group of animals known as **mammals.** Many mammals look very different from each other, but they all have the following in common:

▶ All mammals have fur or hair covering their bodies.

▶ Female mammals have special glands that produce milk to feed their young.

▶ All mammals are **warm-blooded,** which means they keep their body temperature the same at all times.

▶ Mammals have backbones with a **spinal cord.**

▶ Mammals use lungs to breathe air.

Mammals live in many different habitats.

Almost all mammals give birth to live babies. The platypus and the echidna are the only two mammals that lay eggs.

Keywords
• mammals
• warm-blooded
• spinal cord

THE UNITED STATES
Washington, D.C.

Capitol Building

Washington, D.C., the capital of the United States, lies between Virginia and Maryland. Its name honors **George Washington,** the first American president.

Here are some of the places to see in Washington.

Site	What You'll Find There
Capitol Building	Congress meets here.
Supreme Court	The nine Supreme Court justices work here. Above the building's main entrance are the words *Equal Justice Under Law*.
White House	The president and family live at 1600 Pennsylvania Avenue.
Washington Monument	This 555-foot-tall building celebrates George Washington.
Jefferson Memorial	This building contains a statue of **Thomas Jefferson**. It honors the third U.S. president and highlights his writings, including the Declaration of Independence.
Lincoln Memorial	This building contains a statue of **Abraham Lincoln**, the 16th U.S. president, and highlights his famous speeches, including the **Gettysburg Address**.

Keywords
- Washington, D.C.
- George Washington
- Thomas Jefferson
- Abraham Lincoln
- Gettysburg Address

A capital is the *city* where the government of a nation or state meets.
A capitol is the *building* where the government meets.

Social Studies

LIFE SCIENCE
Metamorphosis

Some animals go through different stages of
development during their life cycle, a process
called **metamorphosis.** There are two types of
metamorphosis.

▶ **Complete metamorphosis** has four stages:
egg, larva, pupa, and **adult.** The larva looks
totally different from the adult. During the
pupa stage, the animal changes form.

▶ **Incomplete metamorphosis** has three
stages: egg, **nymph**, and adult. The nymph
almost looks like a miniature adult, with
slightly different body parts.

Nasute termites
(incomplete metamorphosis)

Monarch butterfly
(complete
metamorphosis)

In addition to insects, some amphibians, including
frogs, go through metamorphosis.

Keywords
- metamorphosis
- egg
- larva
- pupa
- adult
- nymph

HELPSTER

11

A Growing Nation

In 1776, the United States had 13 states. By 1959—183 years later—the nation had 50 states.

▶ Many colonists moved west as soon as they could. When enough people lived in an area, it became a new state.

▶ In 1803, the **Louisiana Purchase** doubled the size of the United States when President **Thomas Jefferson** bought the territory from France.

▶ In the middle of the 1800s, many Americans moved west to the Pacific coast. More and more new states joined the nation.

▶ At the same time, land that had been part of Mexico became part of the United States.

▶ In 1959, **Alaska** and **Hawaii** became the last two states.

The United States is still a growing nation. In 1900, our population was 76,212,168. In 2000, its population was 281,421,906. In 2006, America's population reached 300,000,000. What do you think it will be in the year 2100?

Keywords
- Louisiana Purchase
- Thomas Jefferson
- Alaska
- Hawaii

Social Studies

LIFE SCIENCE
Life Cycle of an Animal

All animals go through four main stages in their life cycle. These include **birth, growth, reproduction,** and **death.**

Birth: All animals are born. Some hatch from eggs and others are born live from their mothers.

Growth: Most animals go through different stages of growth when their bodies get bigger and undergo changes.

Reproduction: At some point, animals become mature enough to mate and reproduce, producing offspring that will carry on the species.

Death: Eventually, all animals stop living and die.

Animals have different **life spans.** Some live only a few days, while others can live more than 100 years.

Keywords
- birth
- growth
- reproduction
- death
- life spans

✳HELPSTER

The American Flag

The **American flag** is the country's most important patriotic symbol. It represents all that the nation stands for. You show your respect for the flag and the nation by treating the flag correctly and by saying the **Pledge of Allegiance**.

You show respect for the flag by:

▶ Standing and saluting the flag with your right hand over your heart.

▶ Saying the Pledge of Allegiance:
I pledge allegiance to the Flag of the United States of America, and to the Republic for which it stands, one Nation under God, indivisible, with liberty and justice for all.

The stars stand for the states. A new star is added whenever a new state joins the United States. Today there are 50 stars.

The flag's 13 stripes stand for the 13 original colonies.

Social Studies

The original Pledge of Allegiance was written in 1892 to celebrate the 400th anniversary of Columbus's voyage to America.

Keywords
• American flag
• Pledge of Allegiance

✳HELPSTER

28

LIFE SCIENCE
Parts of an Animal

Animals have different **organs** that work together in systems. While the organs in different animals look different, most animals have three basic systems.

▶ **Circulatory System:** The heart pumps blood through special vessels carrying food and oxygen to all the different cells of the body.

▶ **Nervous System:** The brain uses nerves to gather information from different senses and controls the rest of the systems of the body.

▶ **Skeletal System:** The skeleton gives the body support and works with the muscles to allow an animal to move.

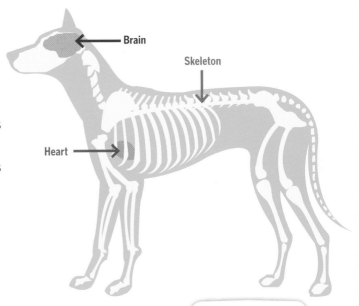

Brain

Skeleton

Heart

Some animals, such as humans, have a skeleton on the inside of their body. Others, such as ladybugs, have it on the outside.

Keywords
- organs
- circulatory system
- nervous system
- skeletal system

✳HELPSTER

"The Star-Spangled Banner"

The **national anthem**—the official song—of the United States is about its flag. The song honors both the flag and the nation.

Francis Scott Key wrote "The Star-Spangled Banner" about a flag he saw during a battle in the War of 1812. (This was another war between Great Britain and the United States.)

The most famous verse is the first verse.

Oh, say, can you see, by the dawn's early light,
What so proudly we hailed at the twilight's last gleaming?
Whose broad stripes and bright stars, through the perilous fight,
O'er the ramparts we watched, were so gallantly streaming?
And the rockets' red glare, the bombs bursting in air,
Gave proof through the night that our flag was still there.
Oh, say, does that star-spangled banner yet wave
O'er the land of the free and the home of the brave?

In 1931, Congress made "The Star-Spangled Banner" the official national anthem.

Keywords
• national anthem
• Francis Scott Key

Social Studies

HELPSTER

29

Life Cycle of a Plant

In order to grow, plants need sunlight, air, and water. When they are ready to reproduce, plants grow flowers and new seeds form in a four-step process.

1. Flower Growth

When flowers form, they contain **pollen** and an **ovary.** The ovary contains the plant's egg cells.

2. Fertilization

Wind, insects, and birds carry the pollen from one flower to the ovary of another. When pollen reaches an ovary, the eggs inside are fertilized.

3. Fruit Growth

After **fertilization,** the ovary ripens to become a fruit and the flower falls off the plant.

4. Seed Growth

Seeds form inside the fruit. Each seed has a baby plant inside called an **embryo.**

Keywords
- pollen
- ovary
- fertilization
- embryo
- germinate

Seeds will only grow, or **germinate,** if the soil conditions are right.

The Statue of Liberty

The **Statue of Liberty** is a famous symbol of the United States. A gift from the people of France, it was completed in 1886. The statue stands in New York Harbor.

▶ The statue's real name is *Liberty Enlightening the World*. It shows a woman holding a torch in one hand and a tablet (book) in the other.

▶ *July 4, 1776* is written on the tablet. The date honors the birth of the United States as a symbol of liberty.

▶ French sculptor **Frédéric-Auguste Bartholdi** designed the statue. He may have used his mother as a model.

▶ The Statue of Liberty stands on Liberty Island, in New York Harbor. It is near **Ellis Island**, which was the first stop for many immigrants to the United States. "Lady Liberty" welcomed them to this land of freedom.

Social Studies

Lady Liberty was built in France then taken apart. It was shipped to the United States in 350 pieces. Small contributions from 120,000 schoolchildren and other Americans funded the building of the statue's base.

Keywords
- Statue of Liberty
- Frédéric-Auguste Bartholdi
- Ellis Island

HELPSTER

30

LIFE SCIENCE
Parts of a Plant

Plants have several different parts to help them grow and reproduce. Each part does a different job.

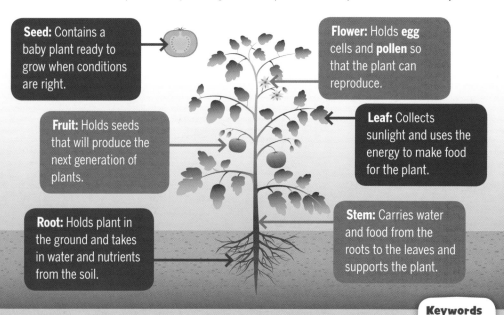

Seed: Contains a baby plant ready to grow when conditions are right.

Flower: Holds **egg** cells and **pollen** so that the plant can reproduce.

Fruit: Holds seeds that will produce the next generation of plants.

Leaf: Collects sunlight and uses the energy to make food for the plant.

Root: Holds plant in the ground and takes in water and nutrients from the soil.

Stem: Carries water and food from the roots to the leaves and supports the plant.

A fruit is any part of a plant that holds seeds. A tomato and a kernel of corn are examples of fruits.

Keywords
- plants
- egg
- pollen

Federal Holidays

In the United States, we observe 10 **federal holidays**. Each honors a different person, idea, or event.

Holiday	Date	Reason for Celebration
New Year's Day	January 1	To look forward to a successful year to come
Martin Luther King Day	Third Monday in January	To honor the Rev. Martin Luther King Jr., civil rights leader
Washington's Birthday/ Presidents' Day	Third Monday in February	To honor all past presidents; originally to celebrate the birthday of George Washington, the first U.S. president
Memorial Day	Last Monday in May	To honor those who died in war
Independence Day/ Fourth of July	July 4	To remember the date the nation was born, when the Declaration of Independence was signed on July 4, 1776
Labor Day	First Monday in September	To honor the nation's working people
Columbus Day	Second Monday in October	To remember the landing of Christopher Columbus in the Americas
Veterans Day	November 11	To honor those who served honorably in the U.S. armed forces in wartime or peacetime
Thanksgiving Day	Fourth Thursday in November	To remember the historic harvest festivals celebrated by the Pilgrims and the Native Americans and to give thanks for family and national blessings
Christmas Day	December 25	A Christian holiday celebrating the birth of Jesus

U.S. government buildings such as post offices are closed on federal holidays.

Keyword
• federal holidays

Social Studies

LIFE SCIENCE
Food Chains

In a food chain, energy is passed from producers to consumers as one thing eats the next. There are three main types of consumers in food chains:

▶ **Herbivores:** These are consumers such as cows, squirrels, and rabbits, which eat only plants. They are near the start of a food chain.

▶ **Carnivores:** These are consumers such as lions, sharks, and hawks, which eat only meat. In the ocean, many carnivores eat one another.

▶ **Omnivores:** These are consumers such as bears and humans, which eat both plants and animals. They are near the end of a food chain.

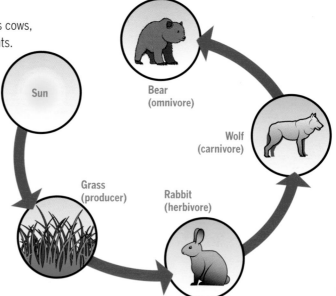

Sun

Bear
(omnivore)

Wolf
(carnivore)

Grass
(producer)

Rabbit
(herbivore)

After animals die, **decomposers** eat them. Their stored energy is released, and a new food chain begins.

Keywords
• herbivores • omnivores
• carnivores • decomposers

Being a Citizen

A **citizen** is a legal member of a nation. Citizens owe loyalty to their nation and are protected by it. U.S. citizens have **rights**, outlined in the Constitution and the laws of the nation. They also have **responsibilities**.

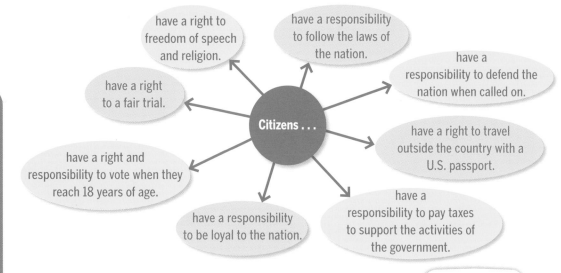

Citizens . . .

have a right to freedom of speech and religion.

have a responsibility to follow the laws of the nation.

have a responsibility to defend the nation when called on.

have a right to a fair trial.

have a right to travel outside the country with a U.S. passport.

have a right and responsibility to vote when they reach 18 years of age.

have a responsibility to be loyal to the nation.

have a responsibility to pay taxes to support the activities of the government.

Celebrate citizenship! September 17—the day the U.S. Constitution was signed—is national Citizenship Day in the United States.

Social Studies

Keywords
• citizen
• rights
• responsibilities

✳HELPSTER

LIFE SCIENCE
Producers

Producers are living things that take energy from the sun or chemicals from inside the earth and turn it into food for themselves, which other living things can use in turn.

On Earth, most of the producers are green plants. In a process called **photosynthesis,** the plants take water, sunlight, and carbon dioxide gas from the air to make simple sugar. They store the sun's energy in their stems, leaves, and fruit. When animals eat plants, they absorb the energy. Animals that eat plants are called **consumers**.

In the ocean, some producers get their energy from chemicals flowing out of the earth, rather than the sun.

Keywords
- producers
- photosynthesis
- consumers

Researching Your Community

You can do **research** to discover information about your community's past, present, and future.

PEOPLE TO INTERVIEW	PLACES TO GO	TOOLS TO USE
▶ Talk to older people to find out about your community's past. Their stories are part of your town's **oral history**. ▶ Interview librarians and other specialists to find out about a particular topic such as government or the environment.	▶ Libraries ▶ Historical societies ▶ Museums ▶ City Hall ▶ Local government agencies	▶ Books ▶ Local newspapers ▶ The Internet ▶ Tape recorders ▶ Cameras and videotape recorders

Check information that you research, to be sure that it is correct.
One good way to do this is to verify every fact in a second source.

Keywords
• research
• oral history

Social Studies

✳HELPSTER

33

Migration

Science

Some animals live their entire lives in one place. Others travel great distances in regular **migrations**. Animals migrate for different reasons.

▶ **For Food:** In the ocean, many animals, including whales, dolphin, and tuna, migrate thousands of miles to find food.

▶ **For Protection from Weather:** As the seasons change, many animals, such as geese and monarch butterflies, migrate to find better climates.

▶ **For Breeding:** Some animals, including salmon and penguins, travel hundreds of miles every year to special **breeding** areas so that they can give birth to their young in a sheltered location.

Scientists believe that some migrating animals use Earth's magnetic field to find their way.

Keywords
• migrations
• breeding

✳HELPSTER

Doing an Oral History

When you do an **oral history**, you ask someone questions about his or her experiences. The better you prepare for your interview, the better the results you will have.

▶ **Do a Pre-Interview:** Contact the person you'll be interviewing and make sure he or she knows a lot about your topic. Also let the person know the types of questions you will ask.

▶ **Be Prepared:** Write down all of the questions you want to ask and go over your list again before the interview. Add any questions you forgot the first time.

▶ **Make Sure Your Equipment Is Working:** Record the interview with a tape recorder or video camera. Make sure you have fresh or fully charged batteries and enough tapes for the whole interview. Test everything before you start.

▶ **Let the Person Talk:** After you ask a question, let your subject answer it. Try not to interrupt. But make sure you get all the information you need. Check your list before you finish and ask any questions that have not been answered.

Be sure to write your interview subject a thank-you note within a few days of the interview.

Social Studies

Keyword
• oral history

HELPSTER

LIFE SCIENCE
Adaptation

An **adaptation** is a special trait that helps a living thing fit in with its surroundings. Animals and plants have many different types of adaptations.

▶ **Structures:** All living things have body parts that help them survive. Polar bears have thick white fur, which protects them from the cold and lets them blend in with the snow. Cacti store water inside their stems, so they do not dry out in the desert heat.

▶ **Behaviors:** Some living things adapt by the way they act. When food becomes scarce in winter, bears **hibernate** (sleep for many weeks) and birds **migrate** to warmer places.

Keywords
- adaptation
- hibernate
- migrate
- evolve

Adaptations don't happen quickly. Organisms **evolve** over thousands of years with useful traits.

✳HELPSTER

Using Time Lines

A **time line** is a diagram that tells you when events happened. Events on a time line are placed in **chronological order**, which means the sequence in time.

▶ You read a horizontal time line from *left to right*. The earliest date is on the left.

When the Colonies Were Founded

1663
North Carolina

1623
New Hampshire

1607
Virginia

1636
Rhode Island

1664
New York

1682
Pennsylvania

1732
Georgia

1600   1625   **1634**   1650   1675   1700   1725   1750
Connecticut

1664
New
Jersey

1682
Delaware

1632
Maryland

1620
Massachusetts

1663
South Carolina

Social Studies

Habitats

Science

Each living thing has its own **habitat**, the environment in which it lives. Different living things **adapt** to different habitats.

Ocean

Oceans are home to a wide range of living things that can survive in salt water. Some things live on the ocean bottom while others swim or float through the water.

Desert

Desert animals and plants must be able to survive with very little water. Some live underground to get away from the heat.

Tundra

Animals and plants that live in the **tundra** must be able to handle cold temperatures and long winters.

Keywords
- habitat
- adapt
- oceans
- desert
- tundra

Other land habitats include forests and grasslands.

2

Using Time Lines (continued)

▶ You read a vertical time line from *top to bottom*. The earliest date is on top.

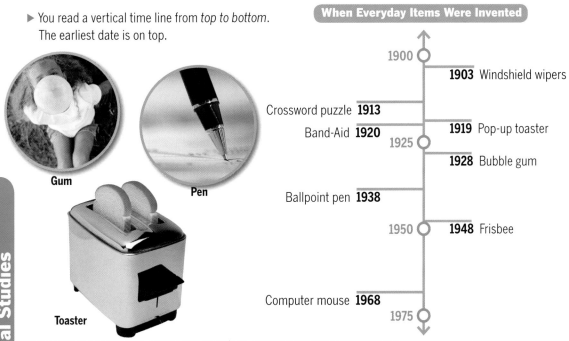

Gum

Pen

Toaster

When Everyday Items Were Invented

1900

1903 Windshield wipers

Crossword puzzle **1913**

Band-Aid **1920**

1925

1919 Pop-up toaster

1928 Bubble gum

Ballpoint pen **1938**

1950

1948 Frisbee

Computer mouse **1968**

1975

Create a vertical or horizontal time line of your own life so far. Start with when you were born. Include items such as the birth of any younger brothers or sisters, your first year in school, when you moved or joined a soccer team, and more.

Keywords
- time line
- chronological order

HELPSTER

36

LIFE SCIENCE
Living or Nonliving?

How do you know if something is living or nonliving? According to scientists, all living things must do the following:

▶ **Grow and Reproduce:** A living thing is born, grows, and dies. When fully grown, it can produce offspring.

▶ **Respond to Stimuli and Move:** A living thing is sensitive and will react to changes in its surroundings, called stimuli.

▶ **Adapt to Its Environment:** A living thing changes to fit in with its environment.

▶ **Obtain Energy:** A living thing needs energy. Plants get their energy from the sun, while animals eat other living things.

Rock

Chair

Nonliving

Insect

Bacteria

Living

Living things are made of cells. Some things have only one cell, while others are made of trillions of cells.

Keywords
• reproduce
• stimuli
• adapt

Using Charts and Graphs

Charts organize information in an orderly way.

▶ A **table** is a type of chart that presents information in categories.

Day	Lunch	Snack
Monday	Tacos	Apples
Tuesday	Tuna salad	Raisins and nuts
Wednesday	Pizza	Frozen yogurt

▶ A **flowchart** shows the order of events in a process.

How to Make a Peanut Butter and Jelly Sandwich

Start with two slices of bread. → Spread peanut butter on one slice. → Spread jelly on the other slice. → Put the slices together. → Cut the sandwich in half. → Eat and enjoy!

Science **Keywords** (continued)

Using Charts and Graphs (continued)

Graphs are drawings that compare quantities.

Our Team's Hits

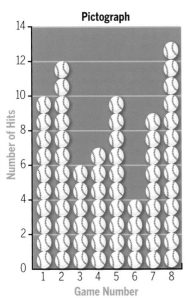

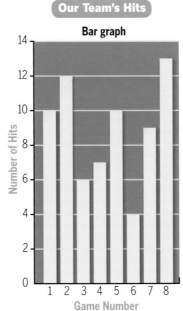

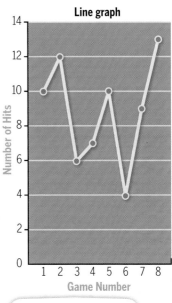

To use a graph, you must read horizontal information—along the bottom or top of the graph—and vertical information—along the side.

Keywords
- charts
- table
- flowchart
- graphs
- pictograph
- bar graph
- line graph

Science Keywords

abdomen	17	climate	31	exoskeleton	17	growth	10
acid rain	30	cold-blooded	14, 15, 16	extinct	18	habitat	2, 19
adapt	1, 2, 18	colony	17	fault	27	herbivore	6
adaptation	3	compass	39	feather	13	hibernate	3
adult	11	constellation	35	fertilization	8	humidity	31
aftershock	27	consumer	5	fish	16	humus	26
aging	20	contaminated	30	flexibility	22	hygiene	23
amphibian	15	crescent	34	food group	21	ice cap	28
anemometer	31	crust	27	force	38	igneous	24
atom	36	death	10	fossil	18	inexhaustible	
axis	33	decomposer	6	friction	38	resource	29
barometer	31	desert	2	full moon	34	invertebrate	17
bird	13	development	20	galaxy	35	larva	11
birth	10	disease	23	gas	36	life span	10
breeding	4	egg	7, 11	geologist	24	liquid	36
carnivore	6	electrical	37	germ	23	liter	40
cartilage	16	embryo	8	germinate	8	loam	26
chemical	37	endangered	19	gill	16	magnetism	38
chemical weathering	25	endurance	22	glacier	28	mammal	12
circulatory system	9	energy	37	gram	40	matter	36
clay	26	evolve	3	gravity	38	mechanical	37

Using the Whole Book

Books are great resources. The lists, pictures, and headings you find in books can help you locate useful information quickly and understand what you read.

Part	Where to Find It	Use It to Learn . . .
Title Page	beginning of the book	the title, author, illustrator, and publisher of a book
Copyright Page	usually at the front of the book	the year a book was published and the publisher's address
Table of Contents	on one of the first few pages after the copyright page	how the book is organized; where to find specific content
Illustrations (maps, photographs, diagrams, graphs, or other pictures)	throughout the book	visual information about a topic (Be sure to read an illustration's **caption**.)
Glossary	at the back of the book (Use the table of contents to locate it.)	difficult words the author uses; new vocabulary specific to the topic
Gazetteer	at the back of the book (Use the table of contents to locate it.)	geographical information about places covered in the book
Index	at the back of the book (Find the page number at the end of the table of contents.)	where to find information on key subjects

Social Studies

Keywords
- caption
- glossary
- gazetteer
- index

Science Contents (continued)

Taking Notes

Taking notes is a good way to help you remember what you have read or what you have heard in class.

▶ Use notes to summarize what you have learned. Write down the most important names and details. Write the big ideas in your own words.

Many Pilgrims came to America to find the freedom to practice their religion.

▶ Use notes to remember keywords. These are the important names and ideas.

Oceanus Hopkins, child born on the Mayflower
Samoset and Squanto, American Indians who helped the Pilgrims

▶ Use notes to keep track of what happened when.

1620 Pilgrims landed in Massachusetts
1621 Gave thanks for survival and a good harvest

▶ Always use quotation marks when you copy exactly what someone else has written!

From <u>The Pilgrims of Plimoth</u> by Marcia Sewall:
"Aye, Governor Bradford calls us pilgrims."

Abbreviations make note-taking simpler. You can use common ones or make up your own. Just make sure you know what they stand for. Some examples: & or + for *and*; w/ for *with*; RR for *railroad*; lib for *library*; hr for *hour*; sec for *second*.

Keywords
• taking notes
• abbreviations

Social Studies

✳HELPSTER

Science Contents

Math Contents

$$\begin{array}{r} 5 \\ \times\,3 \\ \hline 15 \end{array}$$

THE WRITING PROCESS
Writing Letters

Everyone needs to write letters once in a while. Perhaps you want to send your best friend a letter from camp. Every letter contains the same basic parts. Take a look at the friendly letter below.

Always start with a **greeting**. Include the name of the person to whom you are writing.

Dear Rodney,

Skateboarding camp is awesome! Every day I learn new tricks and moves. Yesterday I finally learned how to do a kickflip. Of course, I fell a few times at first. Good thing I was wearing kne

How are you doing? I hope it isn't too hot at h can't wait to see you!

Put your message in the **body** of your letter.

In the **closing**, write your name and an expression of how you feel about the person.

Your friend,

Susan

P.S. Did you remember to water my plant?

Use a **postscript** to add something you forgot.

Keywords
- greeting
- body
- closing
- postscript

Follow these letter-writing rules when writing an e-mail, too. And remember to read over your e-mail to check for mistakes before you click SEND.

HELPSTER

Math Contents (continued)

THE WRITING PROCESS
Publishing

After working so hard, it's important to put the finishing touches on your final version and share it with your teacher, family, or friends. Make sure your work has:

▶ a **title** that accurately summarizes what the work is all about.

▶ your name on the front page or cover sheet. Make sure you get credit for all the work that you did.

▶ any **graphics** you have chosen to use. Graphics are a great way of displaying information. Include your sources—where you got the images or the information displayed in your graphs or charts.

Also remember to fasten the pages together carefully, or place them in a binder. Then congratulate yourself for a job well done.

Why I Like Dogs, by ME

If you really like something you've written, keep it in a safe place. Lots of successful authors remember a particular story they wrote in elementary school that made them decide to pursue a writing career!

Keywords
• title
• graphics

Math **Keywords**

Editing (continued)

Here are some examples using the proofreading marks on the previous page. You can also look online or in a dictionary for a more complete listing of proofreading marks.

Dogs make ^very good pets.

Dogs ~~don't~~ give lots of love.

Dogs are fun to play with. # In conclusion, consider getting a dog.

Dogs love to ride in cars ⊙

Dogs are loyal ^ friendly ^ and loving.

(CAP) some people think they don't li ke dogs, but they sh ould give them a try.

I got my Đog Ƒrom the animal shelter. (lc)

Ask a friend or family member to help you edit and proofread. Often, a person who has never seen the material before can catch mistakes that you miss.

Keywords
• editing
• proofreading marks

Math **Keywords** (continued)

THE WRITING PROCESS
Editing

Nice job! You **improved** your spelling!

Editing is the next step after revising. When you edit, you make sure the words and sentences you use sound good. You also make sure your grammar, spelling, and punctuation are correct. To edit, ask yourself the following questions:

▶ Does my writing sound good when I read it aloud? Have I varied the kinds of sentences I use? Or does every sentence begin the same way?

▶ Have I used words correctly? Have I spelled words correctly?

▶ Have I used the correct grammar, capitalization, and punctuation? For instance, have I capitalized all proper nouns?

You can use **proofreading marks** as you edit. To see examples of the marks in use, turn to the next page.

insert ∧	begin new paragraph ⌗	add comma ⌄	make lowercase / ⓛⓒ
delete ⸙	add period ⊙	capitalize ≡ ⒸⒶⓅ	close up space ⌣

Whole Numbers

Whole numbers can be shown with models.

Look at these **base ten block** models.

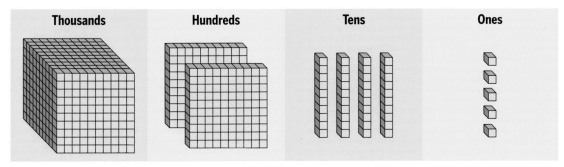

Thousands	Hundreds	Tens	Ones

To find what number the model shows, count how many boxes are in each model, going from left to right.

READ "One thousand, two hundred, forty-five."

WRITE 1,245.

Whole numbers can be written two more ways: *Twenty-eight* is the **word form** for 28. The **standard form** for twenty-eight is 28.

Keywords
- whole numbers
- base ten block
- word form
- standard form

Math

THE WRITING PROCESS
Revising

After finishing your **first draft**, the next step is **revising**. Revising means going back and rewriting or fixing parts of your draft. To revise your work, ask yourself these questions:

▶ Do my introduction and conclusion grab the reader's attention?

▶ Does everything make sense?

▶ Does the order seem logical?

▶ Do I support my ideas with facts and details?

▶ Have I included all the information I need?

▶ Do I go into enough detail about facts and ideas?

If you answer *no* to any of these questions, rewrite to fix the problem. When you are done revising, ask the questions again. Keep going until you can answer *yes* to all of them.

Another person's input can be very helpful. Have a friend or family member read your draft or your first revision. Give that person the list of questions. Have him or her use it to give you feedback.

Keywords
• first draft
• revising

✳HELPSTER

Place Value

Place value tells you the value of each digit in a number.
Digits are the numbers 0, 1, 2, 3, 4, 5, 6, 7, 8, and 9.

From right to left, the first four place values are ones, tens, hundreds, and thousands.
A **period** is each three-digit group in a number. Periods are separated by commas.

Thousands Period			Ones Period		
Hundreds	Tens	Ones	Hundreds	Tens	Ones
		1 ,	7	8	8

Word form: One thousand, seven hundred eighty-eight

Standard form: 1,788

Each place is ten times greater than the place to its right.
So 100 is 10 times greater than 10.

Keywords
- place value
- digits
- period

Math

2

THE WRITING PROCESS
Drafting

Drafting means using your outline and notes to write a first, or rough, draft. For this draft, don't worry too much about things like grammar, punctuation, and spelling. Instead, focus on the big picture. Make sure you include all the information you put in your outline. A good **first draft** has all of the following:

▶ **A thesis:** This is the central, or main, idea of your report. All the other ideas in the report are there to support the **thesis**.

▶ **More than one paragraph:** Each new paragraph is indented. Most paragraphs will have a topic sentence followed by sentences containing supporting facts, details, or explanations. Start a new paragraph when a new idea is introduced.

▶ **A logical sequence of paragraphs:** The introduction, or introductory paragraph, states the thesis. **Supporting paragraphs** give orderly details that support the thesis. The **conclusion**, or concluding paragraph, wraps things up.

Introduction

Supporting paragraphs

Conclusion

Don't reread very much as you write your first draft. It will slow you down. Instead, just concentrate on getting all your information into your draft. There will be time later to make changes.

Keywords
• first draft
• thesis
• supporting paragraphs
• conclusion

Expanded Notation

Expanded notation, also known as **expanded form**, is a method of writing a number to show the value of each digit.

As of the 2000 census, the city of Williamsburg, Virginia, had a total population of 11,998.

Each digit represents a place:

The first 1 stands for 10 thousands =	10,000.
The second 1 stands for 1 thousand =	1,000.
The first 9 stands for 9 hundreds =	900.
The second 9 stands for 9 tens =	90.
The 8 stands for 8 ones =	8.

In expanded notation, 11,998 is written
10,000 + 1,000 + 900 + 90 + 8.

The digit 0 is a place holder. Do not forget it when switching a number from expanded notation to standard form. 908 in expanded notation is 900 + 8.

Keywords
- expanded notation
- expanded form

Math

THE WRITING PROCESS
Getting Organized

Once you've finished prewriting, you need to get organized. Here's how.

▶ Based on your prewriting, write a rough **outline** for your project. List the main topic of your paper. Also list the **thesis**, or most important idea about that topic. For nonfiction, make sure you outline plans for an introduction, supporting paragraphs, and a conclusion. For fiction, list the characters, setting, plot, and theme.

▶ Use the outline to **organize information**. Go through your notes. Next to each piece of information, write where in the outline you would use it. (Use colored flags to indicate different sections of the outline if it helps.) If you want, write each piece of information from your notes on separate index cards. Then divide the cards into stacks based on your outline.

▶ If you are writing nonfiction, decide what visuals you want to include. Would a graph help show information? Would a time line allow readers to better follow events? Separate out the notes you need to create the visuals.

You can write your outline and organize your notes on a computer. Create your own database by typing an outline and adding information from your notes to each section.

Keywords
• outline
• thesis
• organize information

Comparing Whole Numbers

Susan has 384 pennies. Nicholas has 359 pennies. Who has more pennies?

You can use a place-value chart to compare numbers.

Ones Period		
Hundreds	Tens	Ones
3	8	4

Reading from left to right, compare digits starting at the greatest place.

3 hundreds are equal to 3 hundreds.

8 tens are greater than 5 tens.

So, Susan has more pennies than Nicholas.

Ones Period		
Hundreds	Tens	Ones
3	5	9

You can use the symbols $>$, $<$, and $=$ to compare numbers.

$>$ means **is greater than**: $132 > 115$.

$<$ means **is less than**: $815 < 832$.

$=$ means **is equal to**: $210 = 210$.

A whole number with more places than another number will always be greater: 275 is greater than 68.

Keywords
- is greater than
- is less than
- is equal to

Math

4

Taking Notes	Keeping a Log
Taking notes is a useful prewriting tool for a research report. As you do research, take notes on what you find. Later, you can organize the notes before you begin writing.	Keeping a **log** is a good prewriting tool for stories and essays. Record your thoughts and observations in the log for several days. Then look over what you have written. Do any ideas or opinions pop out at you?

My Log

When you do research for a report, make sure you check several different sources. That way, you can be sure your facts are accurate. This is especially important when you use the Internet. Not all Internet sites are written by experts, and many contain errors.

Keywords
- brainstorming
- freewriting
- time line
- character web
- charts
- log

✳HELPSTER

42

Ordinal Numbers

Ordinal numbers tell the **position** or order of objects.

The kid who runs fastest in a race is in first place. The next student is in second place, followed by runners in the third, fourth, fifth, sixth, seventh, eighth, ninth, and tenth places.

The first ten ordinal numbers are:	The next ten ordinal numbers are:
First	Eleventh
Second	Twelfth
Third	Thirteenth
Fourth	Fourteenth
Fifth	Fifteenth
Sixth	Sixteenth
Seventh	Seventeenth
Eighth	Eighteenth
Ninth	Nineteenth
Tenth	Twentieth

Remember, *ordinal* numbers tell the *order* of things.

Keywords
- ordinal numbers
- position

Math

5

THE WRITING PROCESS
Prewriting

Writing a story, essay, or report is a process. Prewriting is the first step in that process. It's what you do before you even know what you are going to write. Below are some different types of prewriting.

Brainstorming	Freewriting	Using Graphic Organizers
Brainstorming means making a list of everything that comes to mind about a particular topic. Don't stop to think about whether the ideas are good or bad. Just write them down.	**Freewriting** means writing about whatever comes into your mind for a set number of minutes. It works especially well for writing with no assigned topic. After you finish freewriting, read what you wrote. Can you find an idea for a story, an essay, or a report?	Graphic organizers can help you organize your thoughts about a topic. They are useful for stories and essays with assigned topics. A **time line** can help you organize events for a narrative. A **character web** can help you organize your thoughts about a story character. **Charts** can help you organize facts for a report.

Odd and Even Numbers

Even numbers have 0, 2, 4, 6, or 8 in the ones place. Even numbers are divided evenly by 2.

Odd numbers have 1, 3, 5, 7, or 9 in the ones place. Odd numbers can't be divided evenly by 2.

These numbers follow a pattern in **addition**, **subtraction**, **multiplication**, and **division**.

Addition	
2 + 6 = 8	even + even = even
1 + 7 = 8	odd + odd = even
4 + 9 = 13	even + odd = odd
9 + 2 = 11	odd + even = odd

Subtraction	
12 − 4 = 8	even − even = even
15 − 1 = 14	odd − odd = even
6 − 3 = 3	even − odd = odd
11 − 8 = 3	odd − even = odd

Multiplication	
4 × 2 = 8	even × even = even
3 × 5 = 15	odd × odd = odd
8 × 7 = 56	even × odd = even
7 × 2 = 14	odd × even = even

Division	
16 ÷ 4 = 4	even ÷ even = even
14 ÷ 2 = 7	or odd
33 ÷ 11 = 3	odd ÷ odd = odd
6 ÷ 3 = 2	even ÷ odd = even

These rules help check your work. Say you added 14 + 11 and your answer was 26. Since an even number plus an odd number always gives an odd sum, you know your answer is incorrect.

Keywords
- even numbers
- odd numbers
- addition
- subtraction
- multiplication
- division

Math

✳HELPSTER

6

THE WRITING PROCESS
Writing Process Flowchart

Follow these steps to become a good writer!
(Learn more about them on the following pages.)

Prewriting

Drafting   **Revising**   **Editing**   **Publishing**

Getting Organized

NUMBER SENSE AND OPERATIONS
Rounding

To **round** is to change a number to an easier number worth about the same amount.

A baseball stadium seats 12,365 people. How many people can the stadium seat, rounded to the nearest thousand?

LOOK at the digit to the right of the number you're rounding: (3 hundred).

THINK "Is this digit **less than** (<) or **greater than** (>) 5?" (3 < 5).

WRITE zeros for every place to the right of the number you're rounding. Keep that number the same if the digit to the right of it is less than 5. Round up if it is 5 or more. (12,365 rounds to 12,000.)

The stadium seats about 12,000 people.

You can also use a number line to round numbers.

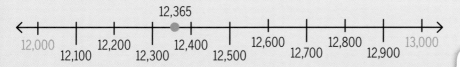

12,365

12,000   12,100   12,200   12,300   12,400   12,500   12,600   12,700   12,800   12,900   13,000

Since 12,365 is closer to 12,000 than 13,000, it rounds to 12,000 when rounded to the nearest thousand.

Math

Keywords
- round
- less than (<)
- greater than (>)

7

NONFICTION
Reference Materials

Reference materials are an important nonfiction genre. Here is a list of common reference materials and how to use them.

Reference Book	What It Is
Dictionary	An alphabetical list of words and their meanings and pronunciations. Use a dictionary to look up unknown words or to check spelling.
Thesaurus	An alphabetical list of words and synonyms for their various meanings. Use a thesaurus to find synonyms. A thesaurus is useful when you want variety in your writing.
Encyclopedia	A book or set of books containing facts about many important topics. Entries are organized alphabetically. Use an encyclopedia to help you research a topic.
Atlas	A book of maps. Use an atlas to look up a country, state, or other place. Atlases can also show you landforms and bodies of water. Some atlases contain information about weather.
Almanac	A collection of facts and statistics, usually about a single country or a certain year. Use an almanac to get up-to-date facts and statistics.

All of these reference books can be found at the library.
Versions of them can also be found online.

Keywords
• dictionary
• thesaurus
• encyclopedia
• atlas
• almanac

Fact Families: Addition and Subtraction

Fact families are groups of related **addition** and **subtraction** facts.

 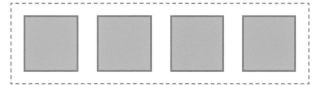

3 + 4 = 7	7 − 3 = 4
4 + 3 = 7	7 − 4 = 3

Addition and subtraction are **inverse** (opposite) **operations**.
Undo one with the other.   5 + 9 = 14   14 − 9 = 5

Keywords
- fact families
- addition
- subtraction
- inverse operations

Math

8

NONFICTION
Fact or Opinion?

Most nonfiction contains both **facts** and **opinions**. It's important to be able to tell them apart. Here's how:

Fact or Opinion?	What It Is	Example
Fact	A statement that can be proven true	The USA has 50 states.
Opinion	A statement of what someone thinks, feels, or believes. Often it contains signal words like *think, believe, feel, best, worst, always,* or *never*.	Hawaii is the most beautiful state in the nation.

Sometimes, in advertisements or other writing, opinions are presented as facts. It's important to know the difference. When reading nonfiction, especially ads, ask yourself the following questions:

▶ Can the statements made be proven true?

▶ Are the statements presenting an opinion as a fact? Does the "fact" contain a word like *best, worst, always,* or *never*? If so, it very well may be an opinion.

Use a newspaper to compare fact and opinion. The articles on the paper's front page should report the facts of a news event. On the editorial page and in the letters to the editor section, writers voice their opinions.

Keywords
• fact
• opinion

Adding Whole Numbers

When you **add** whole numbers, you put them together to make a larger number.

These are the parts of an addition problem:

$$47 \leftarrow \text{addend}$$
$$+ \; 12 \leftarrow \text{addend}$$
$$\overline{ 59} \leftarrow \text{sum}$$

Carrying (regrouping):

$1 \leftarrow$ Carry 1 ten (10 extra ones).

$$38$$
$$+ \; 25$$
$$\overline{ 63}$$

Example	**LOOK** at each pair of digits, moving from right to left (ones, then tens).	
64	**THINK** "What is the sum of each pair of digits?"	1
$+ \; 28$	($4 + 8 = 12$ ones; $6 + 2 = 8$ tens)	64
$\overline{?}$	**WRITE** the sums below each pair, carrying a 1 to the next pair for sums greater than 9.	$+ \; 28$
		$\overline{ 92}$

Estimate sums by rounding. If the estimate is close to the real answer, then you know that your answer is reasonable. 700 is close to 713, so the answer is reasonable.

$$436 \qquad 400$$
$$+ \; 277 \qquad + \; 300$$
$$\overline{ 713} \qquad \overline{ 700}$$

Keywords
- add
- addend
- sum
- carrying

Math

Glossary

Like an index, a **glossary** is found at the back of a book. A glossary, too, is arranged in **alphabetical order**. A glossary is a mini-dictionary just for a single book. It lists and defines important or hard words from the book.

Glossary words are listed alphabetically.

Glossary

Fakie: Riding a skateboard backward, with your feet positioned opposite to the way they usually are.

Each word in the glossary is defined.

Heelflip: Kicking the skateboard with the heel of your front foot to make it spin while you are in the air. Similar to a kickflip, but in the opposite direction.

Kickflip: Kicking the skateboard with the ball of your front foot to make it spin while you are in the air. Similar to a heelflip, ~~but~~ ~~the oppos~~ite direction.

Some definitions will include pronunciations, as in a dictionary.

Ollie (AH-lee): Popping the ~~skateboard while ri~~ding it. This is the basis for all skateboard tricks.

A glossary is the first place to look when you come across an unknown word while reading. Glossaries can also help you remember new words that appear often in a book.

Keywords
- glossary
- alphabetical order

Properties of Addition

Addition is the joining of two or more sets. The numbers that are added are the **addends**. The answer to an addition problem is the **sum**.

The **Commutative Property of Addition** shows that the order of the addends does not change the sum. For example,

$$3 + 9 = 9 + 3.$$

The **Associative Property of Addition** shows that the way the addends are grouped does not change the sum. You can add them in any order. For example,

$$4 + (6 + 7) = (4 + 6) + 7.$$
(Add the numbers in parentheses first.)

The **Identity Property of Addition** states that when 0 is added to another addend, the sum is the other addend. For example,

$$5 + 0 = 5.$$

Keywords
- addends
- sum
- Commutative Property of Addition
- Associative Property of Addition
- Identity Property of Addition

The Associative Property of Addition makes adding easier. You can group addends different ways. Look for addends that add up to easy numbers like 10. Add them first.

$5 + 7 + 3$
$5 + (7 + 3)$
$5 + 10 = 15$

Math

⚹HELPSTER

10

Index

An **index** is found at the back of a nonfiction book. It lists all the topics, or subjects, discussed in the book. The topics are arranged in **alphabetical order**. An index also lists the pages where each topic is discussed.

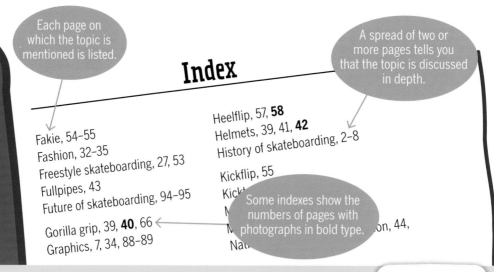

Each page on which the topic is mentioned is listed.

A spread of two or more pages tells you that the topic is discussed in depth.

Index

Fakie, 54–55
Fashion, 32–35
Freestyle skateboarding, 27, 53
Fullpipes, 43
Future of skateboarding, 94–95

Gorilla grip, 39, **40**, 66
Graphics, 7, 34, 88–89

Heelflip, 57, **58**
Helmets, 39, 41, **42**
History of skateboarding, 2–8

Kickflip, 55
Kick...
M...
M...on, 44,
Nat...

Some indexes show the numbers of pages with photographs in bold type.

When doing research, try looking at a book's index before you read the book. The index can tell you right away if this book will be useful.

Keywords
• index
• alphabetical order

✳HELPSTER

36

Subtracting Whole Numbers

Subtraction tells you how many are left when some are taken away.

These are the parts of a subtraction problem: ⟶

$$497 \leftarrow \text{minuend}$$
$$- 123 \leftarrow \text{subtrahend}$$
$$374 \leftarrow \text{difference}$$

Borrowing (regrouping): ⟶

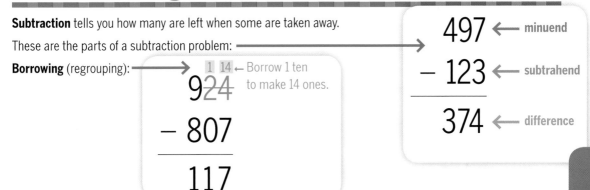

1 14 ← Borrow 1 ten to make 14 ones.

$$9\overset{1}{2}\overset{14}{4}$$
$$- 807$$
$$117$$

Example	**LOOK** at each pair of digits, moving from right to left (ones, tens, hundreds).	2 15 ← Borrow 1 ten to make 15 ones.

$$935$$
$$- 807$$
$$?$$

LOOK at each pair of digits, moving from right to left (ones, tens, hundreds).

THINK "What is the difference between each pair?" ($15^* - 7 = 8$; $2 - 0 = 2$; $9 - 8 = 1$)

WRITE the differences below the line.

* Remember to borrow 1 from the next digit to the left when a digit in the subtrahend is larger than the digit above it (in the minuend). Borrow 1, add 10.

$$9\overset{2}{3}\overset{15}{5}$$
$$- 807$$
$$128$$

Check a subtraction answer by adding the difference and the subtrahend. If the sum is equal to the minuend, the answer is correct.

$$\overset{1}{1}28$$
$$+ 807$$
$$935$$

Keywords
- subtraction
- borrowing
- minuend
- subtrahend
- difference

Math

⋇HELPSTER

11

NONFICTION
Table of Contents

A **table of contents** is found near the front of a book. It lists the titles of all the **chapters** in the book. It also lists the page number on which each chapter begins. Use the table of contents to find a chapter in a book or to preview a book. Read all the chapter titles and make predictions about what you'll find inside.

Table of Contents

Chapter 1—What Is a Skateboard? 3

Chapter 2—How Skateboarding Began 11

Chapter 3—Skateboarding Stars 25

Chapter 4—How to Skateboard Safely 34

Chapter 5—Where to Skateboard 46

Chapter 6—Skateboarding Tricks 53

Chapter titles are clues to what the chapters will contain.

The page number tells you on which page a chapter begins.

Chapters are always shown in order.

Use tables of contents to help you decide if you want to read a book. If the book is fiction, see if the chapter titles sound exciting. If the book is nonfiction, see if the chapters cover topics that interest you.

Keywords
- table of contents
- chapters

Mental Math

Mental math helps you solve math problems in your head.
Here are two ways to add two 2-digit numbers in your head.

$74 + 45 = ?$

Use Expanded Notation

▶ Add the digits in the tens place ($70 + 40 = 110$).
▶ Next add the digits in the ones place ($4 + 5 = 9$).
▶ Add the tens and ones to find your answer:
  $110 + 9 = 119$.

Round

▶ 74 is close to 70.*
  * Remember you subtracted 4 ones to make 70.
▶ 45 is close to 50.*
  * Remember you added 5 extra ones to make 50.
▶ $70 + 50 = 120$
▶ Adjust for the changes you made to the addends.
  Undo addition with subtraction, and vice versa.
  $120 + 4 - 5 = 119$.

Check your addition by doing the same problem a different way. If you lined up the numbers and carried, add with expanded notation or rounding to check your answer.

Keywords
• mental math
• expanded notation
• round

Math

NONFICTION
Nonfiction Genres

The world of **nonfiction** includes any kind of writing that isn't make-believe. Nonfiction books and articles do not come from a writer's imagination. They are based on facts and information. Here are some of the **genres** of nonfiction.

Genre	What it is	Example
reference book	a book in which you look up useful facts and information	*World Book's Encyclopedia of Flags*
textbook	a book that contains lessons and is often used in school	*McGraw-Hill Language Arts, Grade 3*
nonfiction book	an account of a subject that is made up of facts, not fiction	*The Roman Army: The Legendary Soldiers Who Created an Empire* by Dyan Blacklock
biography	the story of a person's life	*Hammerin' Hank: The Life of Hank Greenberg* by Yona Zeldis McDonough
autobiography, journal, or memoir	a person's life story told in his or her own words	*Bill Peet: An Autobiography*

Remember, if you are writing nonfiction, you can't make things up.

Keywords
• nonfiction
• genres

*HELPSTER

What Is Multiplication?

Multiplication is a shortcut for repeated addition (adding a number to itself).
The numbers being multiplied are **factors**.
Answers are **products**.

These are the parts of a multiplication problem:

$$5 \leftarrow \text{factor}$$
$$\times\ 3 \leftarrow \text{factor}$$
$$\overline{15} \leftarrow \text{product}$$

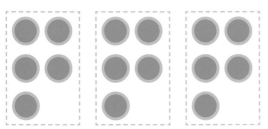

$5 + 5 + 5 = 15$
3 groups of 5 is 15.
$3 \times 5 = 15$

You can think of multiplication as **skip counting**.
To find the product of 2×6, skip count by 2s six times: 2, 4, 6, 8, 10, 12

0 1 2 3 4 5 6 7 8 9 10 11 12 13 14 15 16 17 18 19 20

So $2 \times 6 = 12$.

Keywords
• multiplication
• factors
• products
• skip counting

Math

13

HELPSTER

FICTION AND POETRY
Literary Devices

Poets and writers often use tools, called literary devices, to give readers a better sense of the people and places they're writing about. Here are some common literary devices.

Literary Device	What It Is	Examples
simile	a comparison of two unlike things using the words *like* or *as*	He sang <u>like</u> a frog croaking at dusk. Her smile was <u>as</u> bright <u>as</u> the midday sun.
metaphor	a comparison of unlike things that states one thing as if it were another without using *like* or *as*.	The athlete was a lion—proud, brave, and strong.
repetition	repeating words and phrases	He was happy, so happy, as happy as he had ever been.
alliteration	the repetition of beginning consonant sounds	She sells seashells by the seashore.
onomatopoeia	using words that imitate sounds	The doorbell rang—*ding-dong!*
imagery	descriptions that paint pictures in the mind	The kitchen was warm and bright and cozy. The smell of cookies baking grew stronger with every tick of the oven timer.
rhyme	words or lines that end with similar sounds	Little Jack Horner / Sat in the corner.

Alliteration and rhyme are generally used in poetry. The other literary devices are commonly found in both prose and poetry.

Keywords
- simile
- metaphor
- repetition
- alliteration
- onomatopoeia
- imagery
- rhyme

HELPSTER

Multiplication Table

There are 6 students in each reading group. There are 7 groups of students. How many students are there altogether?

A **multiplication table** can be used to find the **products**.

To use a multiplication table, look at the row that starts with your first **factor** (6). Then look at the column for the number representing the other factor (7). The product of the two numbers is the box where the row meets the column.

So 6 × 7 = 42. There are 42 students altogether.

×	0	1	2	3	4	5	6	7	8	9
0	0	0	0	0	0	0	0	0	0	0
1	0	1	2	3	4	5	6	7	8	9
2	0	2	4	6	8	10	12	14	16	18
3	0	3	6	9	12	15	18	21	24	27
4	0	4	8	12	16	20	24	28	32	36
5	0	5	10	15	20	25	30	35	40	45
6	0	6	12	18	24	30	36	42	48	54
7	0	7	14	21	28	35	42	49	56	63
8	0	8	16	24	32	40	48	56	64	72
9	0	9	18	27	36	45	54	63	72	81

Math

Use the Commutative Property of Multiplication to help you multiply.

If 6 × 7 = 42, then 7 × 6 = 42.

Keywords
- multiplication table
- products
- factor

14

| free verse | Free verse is poetry without rules! It doesn't have to rhyme and it doesn't have to have a certain number of lines or syllables. | This Is Just to Say

I have eaten
the plums
that were in
the icebox

and which
you were probably
saving
for breakfast.

Forgive me
they were delicious
so sweet
and so cold.

—William Carlos Williams |

Keywords
- haiku
- cinquain
- limerick
- free verse

Properties of Multiplication

The **Commutative Property of Multiplication** states that the order of the factors does not change the product:

$$5 \times 3 = 3 \times 5.$$

The **Associative Property of Multiplication** states that the way factors are grouped does not change the product:

$$(4 \times 2) \times 6 = 4 \times (2 \times 6).$$
(Multiply the numbers in parentheses first.)

The **Identity Property of Multiplication** states that when 1 is multiplied by another factor, the product is the other factor:

$$5 \times 1 = 5.$$

The **Zero Property of Multiplication** states that when 0 is multiplied by another factor, the product is 0:

$$7 \times 0 = 0.$$

If you learn these properties, you can more easily memorize the **multiplication table**.

Keywords
- Commutative Property of Multiplication
- Associative Property of Multiplication
- Identity Property of Multiplication
- Zero Property of Multiplication
- multiplication table

Math

✳HELPSTER

FICTION AND POETRY
Types of Poems

There are many different types of poems, including the ones below. However, the most common type of modern poetry is free verse.

Type of Poem	Characteristics	Example
haiku	A haiku has 17 syllables, often in three lines of 5-7-5 syllables.	Catching the sea breeze white wings glide above the waves. Seagulls soar . . . Freedom —Suzanne Honour
cinquain	A cinquain is a five-line poem. The word count for each line is 1-2-3-4-1.	Oven Hot, dark Bakes, broils, burns A cake cooking wonder Stove —Sunita Apte
limerick	A limerick is a funny five-line poem. The first, second, and fifth lines rhyme (and sometimes end in the same words), and the third and fourth lines rhyme.	There was an Old Man of Peru, Who watched his wife making a stew; But once by mistake, In a stove she did bake, That unfortunate Man of Peru. —Edward Lear

Arrays

An **array** is an arrangement of objects, pictures, or numbers in **rows** and **columns**. Multiply the number of rows by the number of columns to find out how many items are in the array.

This array has 3 rows and 4 columns. Each row has 4 stars. Each column has 3 stars.

$3 \times 4 = 12$, so there are 12 stars in the array.

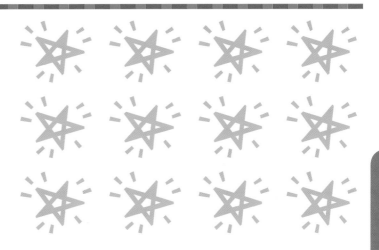

Math

Use arrays to help you divide. $24 \div 4 = ?$ Draw rows of 4 dots until you have 24 of them. How many rows do you have? $24 \div 4 = 6$.

Keywords
• array
• rows
• columns

16

✳HELPSTER

FICTION AND POETRY
Fiction: Plot

The **plot** is the series of events that take place in a story. It has three important parts:
the **conflict**, the **climax**, and the **resolution**.

▶ The conflict is the main problem in the story. The problem can be internal
or external. An internal conflict occurs when a character has problems
deciding what to think or feel. An external conflict occurs when a character
has problems with other characters or with nature.

▶ The climax is the point in the plot when the main character realizes
how he or she can solve the conflict.

▶ The resolution is when a solution to the problem is reached.

Often, a story is told in the order in which things happen. The conflict
is introduced at the beginning. The climax takes place in the middle.
And the resolution takes place at the end.

Keywords
• plot
• conflict
• climax
• resolution

✳HELPSTER

30

Multiplying Larger Numbers

Dr. Allen drives 102 miles to and from work each week. If she works 49 weeks a year, how many miles does she drive in a year?

Step One	Step Two
LOOK at the ones digit in the second **factor** (9).	LOOK at the tens digit in the second factor (4).

Step One

THINK "What is the **product** of 9 and each digit in the first factor (multiplying from right to left)? What is the sum of these products?"
($9 \times 2 = 18$ ones; $9 \times 0 = 0$ tens;
$9 \times 1 = 9$ hundreds; $18 + 0 + 900 = 918$.)

WRITE the two factors on top of each other and the partial product below a line. **Carry** when the product of two digits is greater than 9.

$$\begin{array}{r} 1 \\ 102 \\ \times\ 49 \\ \hline 918 \end{array}$$

Step Two

THINK "What is the product of 4 and each digit in the first factor? What is the sum of these products?"
($4 \times 2 = 8$ ones;
$4 \times 0 = 0$ tens;
$4 \times 1 = 4$ hundreds;
$8 + 0 + 400 = 408$.)

WRITE a 0 in the ones position and the new partial product to its left.

$$\begin{array}{r} 1 \\ 102 \\ \times\ 49 \\ \hline 918 \\ +\ 4,080 \\ \hline 4,998 \end{array}$$
→ Add the two partial products for your answer.

Answer: Dr. Allen commutes 4,998 miles in a year.

You can also use **expanded notation** to multiply large numbers.
$23 \times 4 = ?$
$23 = 20 + 3$ so $23 \times 4 = 20 \times 4 + 3 \times 4 = 80 + 12 = \mathbf{92}$

Keywords
- factor
- product
- carry
- expanded notation

Math

Fiction: Useful Terms

All fiction stories, whether realistic or unrealistic, have the same main parts.

Characters	The characters are the people, animals, or imaginary beings that are in the story. The main character is the most important one in the story.
Setting	The setting is where and when the story takes place. The story can be set in the real world or in an imaginary world. It can take place in the past, present, or future.
Plot	The plot is what happens in the story. For more about plot, see the next page.
Point of View	The point of view depends on who is telling the story. Sometimes, a character in the story is the narrator. The narrator uses the pronoun *I*. This type of story uses first-person point of view. Sometimes the author is the narrator. The narrator refers to all the characters as "he" and "she." This type of story uses third-person point of view.
Theme	A theme is the story is most important message or idea. Usually, the author wants to use the story to give this message to the reader. A theme usually is not stated directly. Readers must figure it out for themselves.

Think about how you use point of view when you write. Which point of view do you use when you write a letter or an e-mail? (probably first person) When do you use third-person point of view? (possibly in a report for school)

Keywords
- characters
- setting
- plot
- point of view
- theme

✳HELPSTER

29

What Is Division?

Division is a shortcut for repeated subtraction. Division breaks up a number into **equal** groups. It also tells you how many times one number (a **divisor**) fits into another one (a **dividend**).

Terrence has 15 counters. He wants to put 3 counters in each bag. How many bags will he need?

$15 \div 3 = 5$. Terrence needs 5 bags.

Now he wants to put 15 counters equally into 5 bags. How many counters will go into each bag?

$15 \div 5 = 3$. Terrence puts 3 counters in each bag.

When you divide by putting objects into groups, make sure you put the same number of objects in each group.

Keywords
- division
- equal
- divisor
- dividend

Math

Fiction Genres

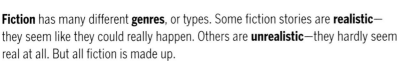

Fiction has many different **genres**, or types. Some fiction stories are **realistic**—they seem like they could really happen. Others are **unrealistic**—they hardly seem real at all. But all fiction is made up.

Genre	Realistic or Unrealistic?	Example
realistic fiction	realistic	*Shiloh* by Phyllis Reynolds Naylor
mystery	realistic	*Cam Jansen* by David Adler
historical fiction	realistic	*Little House on the Prairie* by Laura Ingalls Wilder
fantasy	unrealistic	*Charlotte's Web* by E. B. White
science fiction	unrealistic	*2095 (The Time Warp Trio)* by Jon Scieszka
folktales (including myths, legends, fables, fairy tales, and tall tales)	unrealistic	*The Firebird* by Jane Yolen

Before you settle on one or two favorite types of fiction, read a few books from each genre. Ask your friends, teacher, or local librarian for recommendations.

Keywords
- fiction
- genres
- realistic
- unrealistic

Division Facts

The number that is divided is the **dividend**.
The number you divide by is the **divisor**.
The amount in each group, or the answer, is the **quotient**.

Say you divide 18 by 3.

dividend $\longrightarrow$ $18 \div 3 = 6$ $\longleftarrow$ quotient

$\uparrow$
divisor

18 can be divided into 3 groups of 6.
The quotient (6) is the number of times the divisor (3) fits into the dividend (18).

Math

Multiplication and division are **inverse operations**. You can use
a multiplication fact to learn a division fact. If $4 \times 7 = 28$, then
$28 \div 7 = 4$ and $28 \div 4 = 7$.

Keywords
• dividend
• divisor
• quotient
• inverse operations

HELPSTER

19

SENTENCES AND PUNCTUATION
Abbreviations

Abbreviations are shortened forms of words. Many abbreviations
have periods after them. Many are capitalized.

Type of Abbreviation	Is It Capitalized?	Does It Need a Period?	Examples
a person's title	yes	yes	Mrs. (Missus), Mr. (Mister), Dr. (Doctor), M.A. (Master of Arts)
a location	yes	sometimes	St. (Street), Rd. (Road), MT (Montana), USA (United States of America)
a direction	yes	no	N (north), NW (northwest), E (east), SE (southeast)
a day or month	yes	yes	Tues. (Tuesday), Nov. (November)
a measurement	no	yes	ft. (foot or feet), in. (inch or inches), oz. (ounce or ounces), qt. (quart or quarts)

Most dictionaries have a list of common abbreviations.
If you need help abbreviating a word, look it up!

Keyword
• abbreviations

DIVISION
Long Division

Long division can help you figure out how many times one number fits into another. $112 \div 4 = ?$

Step One

LOOK at the **divisor** (4) and the first digit of the **dividend** (1). 1 is smaller than 4, so look at the first two digits: 11.

THINK "How many times does 4 fit into 11? 2 times."

WRITE the partial **quotient** (2) above the dividend and the product of the divisor and the partial quotient ($4 \times 2 = 8$) under the dividend. Subtract and write the difference below. ($11 - 8 = 3$). Bring down the next digit of the dividend (2).

$$\begin{array}{r} 2 \\ 4\overline{)112} \\ -8\downarrow \\ \hline 32 \end{array}$$

Step Two

LOOK at the divisor (4) and the difference (32).

THINK "How many times does 4 fit into 32? 8 times."

WRITE the partial quotient (8) above the dividend and the product of the divisor and the new partial quotient ($4 \times 8 = 32$) under it. Subtract and write the difference ($32 - 32 = 0$) below. $112 \div 4 = 28$.

$$\begin{array}{r} 28 \\ 4\overline{)112} \\ -8\downarrow \\ \hline 32 \\ -32 \\ \hline 0 \end{array}$$

→ Align the partial quotient (8) with the last number you brought down (2).

→ When you've brought down all digits in the dividend (112), this number (0) is the **remainder**.

When you divide, the remainder is *always* less than the divisor.

Keywords
- long division
- divisor
- dividend
- quotient
- remainder

Math

SENTENCES AND PUNCTUATION
Capital Letters

When should a word begin with a **capital letter**? Follow these general rules to figure it out.

Rules for Capital Letters	Examples
Capitalize the first word of a sentence.	Skateboarding is my favorite sport.
Capitalize the first word of quotations.	I said, "That was the most awesome ride ever!"
Capitalize the pronoun *I*.	The first time I went surfing, I loved it.
Capitalize ALL proper nouns.	My neighbor, Max Quinn, loves surfing, too. I loved surfing at Green Waves Beach.
Capitalize people's titles. Also capitalize family relationships if they come right before a name.	I saw Dr. Ruiz and Mrs. Kim at the beach. I hope Aunt Inez comes to the beach with me. Inez is my favorite aunt.
Capitalize proper adjectives that describe someone's nationality or ethnic background.	Max is African-American, and Dr. Ruiz is Mexican.

With proper nouns, capitalize *the* if it is part of the name. Don't capitalize *the* if it isn't.

• That restaurant is called The Happy Rabbit.

• Have you ever eaten at the Carroll Café?

Keyword
• capital letter

✳HELPSTER

26

Estimating Products and Quotients

An **estimate** is close to an answer, but not exact.

Estimate Products	Estimate Quotients
A stadium has 48 rows with 31 seats in each row. About how many seats are there in the stadium?	A classroom library has 248 books. There are 5 bookcases holding the same number of books. About how many books are in each bookcase?
Round the factors.	Round to **compatible numbers**.
48 rounds to 50.	248 is close to 250, and $25 \div 5 = 5$.
31 rounds to 30.	$250 \div 5 = 50$.
Multiply the rounded numbers: $50 \times 30 = 1,500$.	The library has about 50 books in each case.
There are about 1,500 seats.	

When multiplying whole numbers that end with zeros, remove the zeros to make the multiplication easier. Then put the same number of zeros you removed at the end of the product. $50 \times 30 = ?$ $5 \times 3 = 15$ $50 \times 30 = 1,500$

Keywords
- estimate
- round
- compatible numbers

Math

21

SENTENCES AND PUNCTUATION
Quotation Marks

Quotation marks [**" "**] surround what a person says. Anything in quotation marks is an exact record of someone's words. Only put quotation marks around what a person has said. Any other information should be outside the quotation marks.

exactly what was said   "This looks like a great place to skateboard," Susan said.   **who said it**

▶ Use quotation marks for dialogue in fiction. Always start a new paragraph for a new speaker.

▶ Use quotation marks in nonfiction for things that people said or writing that you take from another source. Always identify the source of your quotation.

▶ Always place commas and periods inside the quotation marks.

Question marks and exclamation points only go inside quotation marks if they are part of the quote. If they are part of a larger sentence, they go outside the quote.

• Susan said, "Wow, that's awesome!"
• Can you believe Susan said, "Wow, that's awesome!"?

Keywords
• quotation marks

What Are Fractions?

A **fraction** describes part of a whole or group. The bottom number, or **denominator**, names the total number of equal parts. The top number, or **numerator**, names the number of parts being described.

What fraction of this figure is shaded?

The figure has 4 equal parts.
The denominator is 4.

3 parts are shaded.
The numerator is 3.

$\frac{3}{4}$ of the figure is shaded.

$$\frac{3}{4}$$ ← numerator

← denominator

When a figure is divided to show fractions, make sure the parts are all the same size.

Keywords
- fraction
- denominator
- numerator

Math

SENTENCES AND PUNCTUATION
Apostrophes

We're closing soon. You can't linger much longer.

An **apostrophe** ['] is used to show where letters are left out in contractions. It is also used to show possession.

Contractions	Possession
'm going skateboarding.	Kenny's ride was amazing.
Susan can't go today.	That skateboard is Susan's
Shouldn't you be doing homework?	Susan s skateboard is very old.

Here are some tricky contractions. Be careful not to confuse them with similar words!

Contraction	Don't Confuse It with . . .	Example Sentences
it's—meaning *it is*	its—the possessive form of *it*	It's a beautiful day today!
		The tree has lost all of its leaves.
they're—meaning *they are*	their—the possessive form of *they*	They re a nice group of students.
		The racers marked their course.
we're—meaning *we are*	were—the past plural form of *is*	We're coming to watch Keisha.
		The racers were happy to have an audience.

Keyword
• apostrophe

Comparing Fractions

Fractions with **common denominators** have the same number in their denominators.

To compare fractions with common denominators, look at the numerators.

Which is less: $\frac{2}{7}$ or $\frac{4}{7}$?

The fraction with the smaller numerator is smaller. $\frac{2}{7} < \frac{4}{7}$ because $2 < 4$.

To compare fractions with **unlike denominators**, you can use a number line.

Which is greater: $\frac{2}{6}$ or $\frac{2}{3}$?

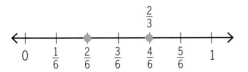

$\frac{2}{6}$ is to the left of $\frac{2}{3}$.

$\frac{2}{3}$ is farther away from 0.

$\frac{2}{3}$ is greater than $\frac{2}{6}$.

If two fractions have the same numerator, the greater fraction is the one with the smaller denominator:
$\frac{2}{5} > \frac{2}{7}$.

Keywords
- common denominators
- unlike denominators

Math

23

✳HELPSTER

SENTENCES AND PUNCTUATION
Commas

A **comma** [,] shows a pause in writing. It is also used to separate words so that readers will not be confused. Here are some common places to use commas.

Use a Comma for . . .	Examples
items in a series (A series is a list of three or more words together in a sentence.)	Red, yellow, and blue are the primary colors. The first, second, third, fourth, and fifth graders all went to the assembly.
locations	San Diego, California, is a long way from London, England!
dates	April 24, 1997, is the date I was born.
the greeting and closing of a letter	Dear Mom, I miss you. Skateboarding camp is awesome! Parents' day is coming up in two weeks. See you then! With love, Susan
addresses	Susan lives at 1518 Wood Drive, Durham, North Carolina.

Keyword
• comma

Adding and Subtracting Fractions

To add fractions with **common denominators**,
add the numerators. The denominator stays the same.

$$\frac{2}{5} + \frac{1}{5} = ?$$

Add the numerators: $2 + 1 = 3$. ⟶

$$\frac{2}{5} + \frac{1}{5} = \frac{3}{5}$$

To subtract fractions with common denominators,
subtract the numerators. The denominator stays the same.

$$\frac{4}{7} - \frac{2}{7} = ?$$

Subtract the numerators: $4 - 2 = 2$. ⟶

$$\frac{4}{7} - \frac{2}{7} = \frac{2}{7}$$

You can check the answer by using an **inverse operation**.
Use subtraction to check addition.

To check $\frac{7}{9} - \frac{5}{9} = \frac{2}{9}$, add: $\frac{2}{9} + \frac{5}{9} = \frac{7}{9}$.

Keywords
- common denominators
- inverse operation

Math

*HELPSTER

24

SENTENCES AND PUNCTUATION
Combining Sentences

Combining sentences means turning two sentences into one.

▶ Sometimes two sentences have the same subject. Sometimes they have the same predicate. In these cases, you can combine two sentences into one.

Sentences	Combined
Susan likes skateboarding. Susan likes surfing.	Susan likes <u>skateboarding and surfing</u>.
Susan likes skateboarding. Kenny likes skateboarding.	<u>Susan and Kenny</u> like skateboarding.

▶ You can use conjunctions to combine two different sentences.

Sentences	Conjunction	Combined
Susan skateboards every day. She's getting much better at it.	and	Susan skateboards every day, <u>and</u> she's getting much better at it.
Susan likes skateboarding. She isn't very good at it.	but	Susan likes skateboarding, <u>but</u> she isn't very good at it.
Do you want to skateboard? Would you rather relax?	or	Do you want to skateboard, <u>or</u> would you rather relax?

Keywords
• combining sentences

Decimals and Fractions

Decimals, like **fractions**, describe part of a whole. A **decimal point** separates the whole-number part (to the left of the decimal point) from the decimal part (to the right).

whole number ⟶ 3.1 ⟵ decimal

You can use models to represent decimals.

This model represents 0.1.	This model represents 0.25.
Decimal: 0.1 Fraction: $\frac{1}{10}$ **READ** "One-tenth."	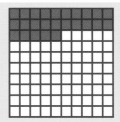 Decimal: 0.25 Fraction: $\frac{25}{100}$ **READ** "Twenty-five hundredths."

You can use a place-value chart to represent decimals. The decimal 39.56 is represented by this place-value chart.

Hundreds Period			Fractions Period		
Hundreds	Tens	Ones	Tenths	Hundredths	Thousandths
	3	9 .	5	6	

Keywords
- decimals
- fractions
- decimal point

Math

25

SENTENCES AND PUNCTUATION
Run-ons and Fragments

A complete sentence contains both a subject and a predicate. **Run-ons** and **fragments** are two common mistakes that people make when writing sentences.

▶ **Run-ons** are sentences that have two complete thoughts not separated by a conjunction. Run-ons usually have two subjects and two predicates but no conjunction. Correct run-ons by adding a conjunction or by making two separate sentences.

Run-on	Add a Conjunction	Make Two Sentences
Susan likes skateboarding I like it, too.	Susan likes skateboarding <u>and</u> I like it, too.	Susan likes skateboarding. I like it, too.

▶ Fragments are incomplete sentences. They are phrases with end punctuation. A fragment lacks either a subject or a predicate. To correct a fragment, first decide what is missing. Then add it. Decide what's missing by asking: *Who or what is this fragment about? What is happening in this fragment?*

Fragment	What Is Missing?	Add It
Likes skateboarding at the park.	a subject	<u>Susan</u> likes skateboarding at the park.
Susan and I	a predicate	Susan and I <u>are going skateboarding</u>.

Keywords
• run-ons
• fragments

Equivalent Fractions

Equivalent fractions have the same value but have different numerators and denominators. They are the same size.

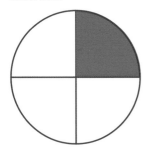

$$\frac{1}{4} = \frac{2}{8}$$

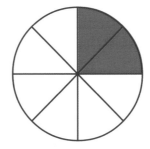

A number line can show fractions *and* equivalent fractions.

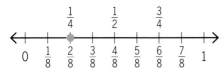

Each mark represents $\frac{1}{8}$.
The three fractions written above $\frac{2}{8}$, $\frac{4}{8}$, and $\frac{6}{8}$ on the number line are equivalent fractions.

To see which fraction is being used, count the number of marks from 0 to 1, but don't include 0. The number of marks is the denominator.

Keywords
• equivalent fractions

Math

26

SENTENCES AND PUNCTUATION
Subject and Predicate

The **subject** of a sentence is usually a noun or pronoun. It is who or what the sentence is about.
The **predicate** tells what the subject is doing, or just what the subject is. The predicate always includes a verb.

▶ To find the subject of a sentence, ask: *Who or what is this sentence about?*
Susan is skateboarding. Who is this sentence about? (Susan—she's the subject.)

▶ To find the predicate of a sentence, ask: *What is the subject of the sentence doing?*
Susan is skateboarding. What is Susan doing? (She is skateboarding. *Is skateboarding* is the predicate.)

▶ Subjects and predicates can be single words or they can be phrases. Subjects can also be singular or plural.

subject   Susan skateboards.   predicate

subject   My friend Susan is a skateboarder.   predicate

subject   My friends skateboard.   predicate

Always make sure the subject and the verb agree.
Singular subjects take singular verbs. Plural subjects take plural verbs.
Susan <u>skateboards</u> every Saturday. My friends <u>skateboard</u> every Saturday.

Keywords
• subject
• predicate

Money

To find the total value of a collection of money:

First find the total value of the **bills**. Then find the total value of the **coins**.

Start with the bill that has the greatest value. Then count the coins, starting with the coin with the greatest value.

| $10.00 | $15.00 $20.00 $25.00 | $26.00 $27.00 $28.00 $29.00 | $29.25 $29.50 $29.75 | $29.80 $29.85 |

Remembering the following facts can help you work with money:

$1.00 = 100 pennies
　　　 = 20 nickels
　　　 = 10 dimes
　　　 = 4 quarters

Math

Keywords
- bills
- coins

*HELPSTER

27

What Is a Sentence?

A **sentence** is a group of words used to tell a complete thought.
There are four types of sentences: **declarative**, **interrogative**, **imperative**, and **exclamatory**. Certain end punctuation goes with each type of sentence.

Type of Sentence	Is Used to . . .	and Ends with . . .
declarative	say something (make a statement) *Susan loves skateboarding.*	a period (.)
interrogative	ask a question *Do you want to go skateboarding?*	a question mark (?)
imperative	order someone to do something *Give me the skateboard.* *Show what you can do!*	a period (.) or an exclamation point (!)
exclamatory	express strong feelings (fear, anger, happiness, surprise . . .) *That ride was amazing!*	an exclamation point (!)

If you're not sure which punctuation mark to use at the end of a sentence, say it out loud. Then use the chart on this page to decide.

Keywords
- sentence
- declarative
- interrogative
- imperative
- exclamatory

✳HELPSTER

MEASUREMENT
Time

Time is measured in **hours**, **minutes**, and **seconds**.
There are analog and digital clocks and watches.
READ "Ten ten or ten minutes after ten." ⟶

How many minutes are there in 3 hours?
1 hour = 60 minutes $3 \times 60 = 180$
There are 180 minutes in 3 hours.

A **calendar** represents days and weeks.

How many days are there in 2 weeks?

Each row represents 1 week.
There are 7 days in 1 week.
$7 \times 2 = 14$ days

Remembering the following facts can help you work with time:
60 seconds = 1 minute   7 days = 1 week
60 minutes = 1 hour   365 days = 1 year
24 hours = 1 day

Keywords
• time
• hours
• minutes
• seconds
• calendar

Math

PARTS OF SPEECH
Adverbs

Adverbs are words that describe verbs and adjectives. Most adverbs describe how, when, or where something is done. Many adverbs end in *-ly*. In fact, you can make many adverbs by adding *-ly* to the end of an adjective.

How	quickly	Susan will ride her skateboard <u>quickly</u>.
When	early	Susan will ride her skateboard <u>early</u>.
Where	here	Susan will ride her skateboard <u>here</u>.

▶ Like adjectives, adverbs also have **comparative** and **superlative** forms.

Adverb	Comparative Form	Superlative Form
early	earlier (notice how the *y* changes to *i* before the *-er*)	earliest (notice how the *y* changes to *i* before the *-est*)
quickly	more quickly	most quickly

▶ Two very common adverb comparatives and superlatives are irregular.

Adverb	Comparative Form	Superlative Form
well	better	best
badly	worse	worst

Not all words that end in *-ly* are adverbs. Some adjectives end in *-ly* as well, including *lonely*, *friendly*, and *lovely*.

Keywords
• adverbs
• comparative
• superlative

MEASUREMENT
Length

Length is the distance from one end of an object to the other end, or the distance between two objects.

You can use metric or customary units to measure length.

Metric Units of Length	Customary Units of Length
1 **decimeter** (dm) = 10 **centimeters** (cm)	1 **foot** (ft.) = 12 **inches** (in.)
1 **meter** (m) = 100 centimeters (cm)	1 **yard** (yd.) = 3 feet (ft.)

You can use a ruler to measure the length of a pencil.

This pencil is 4 inches long.

$\longleftarrow$ 4 inches $\longrightarrow$

You can use a tape measure to
measure the length of a desk.
This desk is 4 feet long.

$\longleftarrow$ 4 feet $\longrightarrow$

Use what you know to convert measurements.
A rope measures 2 meters long. How many centimeters is that?
If 1 meter = 100 centimeters, and there are 2 meters,
then $100 \times 2 = 200$ centimeters.

Keywords
- length
- decimeter
- centimeters
- meter
- foot
- inches
- yard

Math

✳HELPSTER

29

Verbs (continued)

▶ The **future tense** of a regular verb is formed by adding the verb *will* in front of it.
The future tense is the same even in the third person.

Present Tense	Future Tense
talk	will talk
skate	will skate

▶ Some very common verbs have **irregular tenses**.

Verb	Present	Past	Future
be	am / is / are	was / were	will be
have	have / has	had	will have
go	go / goes	went	will go

Keywords
- verb
- present tense
- past tense
- future tense
- irregular tenses

Weight and Mass

A scale is used to measure the **weight**, or heaviness, of an object.
It can also measure the **mass**, or amount of matter, in an object.

In customary units, weight is measured in
ounces, **pounds**, and **tons**.
  1 pound (lb.) = 16 ounces (oz.)
  1 ton (t) = 2,000 pounds (lb.)

1 ounce

1 pound

1 ton

In metric units, mass is measured in **grams**,
kilograms, and **metric tons**.
  1 kilogram (kg) = 1,000 grams (g)
  1 metric ton (t) = 1,000 kilograms (kg)

1 gram

1 kilogram

1 metric ton

The words **weight** and **mass** are often used to describe how heavy
something is. But weight is affected by Earth's gravity; mass is not.
On the moon, an astronaut weighs less than on Earth, but his or her
mass stays the same.

Keywords
- weight
- mass
- ounces
- pounds
- tons
- grams
- kilograms
- metric tons

Math

*HELPSTER

PARTS OF SPEECH
Verbs

A **verb** is a word that tells what a noun does or is.

Susan <u>goes</u> skateboarding. (tells what the noun does)

Susan <u>is</u> a skateboarder. (tells what the noun is)

A verb's **tense** shows when something happens. Verbs have three main tenses: present, past, and future.

▶ The **present tense** of a verb is known as a base verb.
An -s is added to the third-person form.

First Person	Second Person	Third Person
I talk	you talk	he / she / it talks (third person)
we talk	you talk (plural)	they talk

▶ The **past tense** of a regular verb is formed by adding -ed to a base verb. If the base ends in -e, only a -d is added.
The past tense is the same even in the third person.

Present Tense	Past Tense
talk	talked
skate	skated

Capacity

Capacity measures the amount of dry or liquid volume a container holds. Capacity is measured in customary or metric units.

Customary units of capacity are **cups**, **pints**, **quarts**, and **gallons**.

2 cups (c.) = 1 pint (pt.)
2 pints (pt.) = 1 quart (qt.)
4 quarts (qt.) = 1 gallon (gal.)

If a recipe calls for 3 pints of milk, how many cups are needed?

1 pint = 2 cups

$2 \times 3 = 6$

6 cups of milk

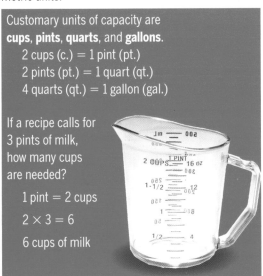

The metric units of capacity are **milliliters** and **liters**.
1,000 milliliters (ml) = 1 liter (l)

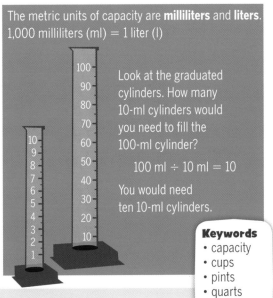

Look at the graduated cylinders. How many 10-ml cylinders would you need to fill the 100-ml cylinder?

$100 \text{ ml} \div 10 \text{ ml} = 10$

You would need ten 10-ml cylinders.

Keywords
- capacity
- cups
- pints
- quarts
- gallons
- milliliters
- liters

Math

To help understand the amount of liquid in one liter, think about drinks in the grocery store sold in one- or two-liter sizes.

Adjectives

Adjectives are words that describe nouns and pronouns. They answer questions such as "What kind?" or "How many?" about a noun. Like nouns, adjectives can be proper or common.

Proper adjectives are made from proper nouns. They always begin with a capital letter. For example: Mexican (from the noun *Mexico*) and English (from the noun *England*). All other adjectives are **common adjectives**. Some common ones are big, small, red, blue, many, and few.

You can use adjectives to compare nouns. To do this, adjectives change form.

▶ **Comparative adjectives** compare two nouns. You can make most comparatives by adding the suffix -*er* to adjectives. For longer adjectives, put the word *more* before them.

▶ **Superlative adjectives** compare more than two. You can make most superlatives by adding the suffix -*est* to adjectives. For longer adjectives, put the word *most* before them.

Adjective	Comparative Form	Superlative Form
fast	faster	fastest
important	more important	most important

Some very common comparatives and superlatives are irregular. For example: good / better / best; bad / worse / worst; much or many / more / most.

Keywords
- adjectives
- proper adjectives
- common adjectives
- comparative adjectives
- superlative adjectives

✳HELPSTER

15

Polygons

A **polygon** is a closed shape made by straight line segments.
Count the number of sides and **angles** (corners) each polygon has.

Triangle	**Square**	**Rhombus**	**Pentagon**	**Trapezoid**	**Hexagon**	**Octagon**

Polygons can be **regular** or **irregular**. If all of its sides have equal lengths, and all angles have equal measures, the polygon is regular.

Regular polygons

Irregular polygons

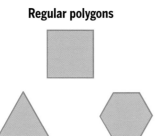

Math

Knowing what these words mean can help you remember how many sides each polygon has: tricycle, quadruped, pentathlon, hexapod, and octopus.

Keywords
- polygon
- angles
- triangle
- square
- rhombus
- pentagon
- trapezoid
- hexagon
- octagon
- regular
- irregular

PARTS OF SPEECH
Pronouns

A **pronoun** is a word that can replace a noun.

Three common types of pronouns are **subject pronouns**, **object pronouns**, and **possessive pronouns**.

Pronoun Type	What It Does	Pronouns	Examples
subject	acts as the subject of a sentence (shows who is doing something)	*I, he, she, it, we, you, they*	<u>Mike</u> washed the car. <u>He</u> washed the car. (The noun *Mike* is replaced by the pronoun *he*.)
object	acts as the object of a sentence (shows to what something is being done)	*me, her, him, it, us, you, them*	Susan washed the <u>car</u>. Susan washed <u>it</u>. (The article and noun *the car* are replaced by the pronoun *it*.)
possessive	shows who owns something	*Mine, hers, his, its, ours, yours, theirs*	That skateboard is <u>Susan's</u>. That skateboard is <u>hers</u>. (*Hers* replaces the noun *Susan's*.)

Keywords
- pronoun
- subject pronouns
- object pronouns
- possessive pronouns

Similar and Congruent

Similar shapes have the same shape, but may be different sizes.

Congruent shapes are exactly the same shape and size.

Congruent shapes are also similar because they have the same shape.

Keywords
- similar
- congruent

Math

✳HELPSTER

PARTS OF SPEECH
Plural Nouns

You can make most nouns **plural** by adding -s to the end.

Singular Noun	Plural Noun
dog	dogs

Some nouns, however, form their plurals in irregular ways.

Nouns Ending in...	How to Make the Plural	Examples
ch, s, sh, x, and *z*	add -es	watch / watches, dress / dresses quiz / quizzes (Here you double the consonant before adding -es.)
f or *fe*	Say the plural form out loud. If you hear an *f* sound, add -s to the word. If you hear a *v* sound, change the *f* or *fe* to *v*. Then add -es.	cliff / cliffs, knife / knives
o	If there is a vowel before the *o*, add -s. If there is a consonant before the *o*, add -es.	radio / radios, potato / potatoes
y	If there is a vowel before the *y*, add -s. If there is a consonant before the *y*, change *y* to *i*. Then add -es.	day / days, party / parties

Some nouns form plurals without adding -s at all: mouse / mice, tooth / teeth, person / people. Other nouns don't change in the plural: shrimp / shrimp, sheep / sheep, deer / deer.

Keywords
• plural nouns

13

Symmetry

A figure has **symmetry** if it can be folded on a line so that both sides match. A **line of symmetry** is the line on which the figure is folded.

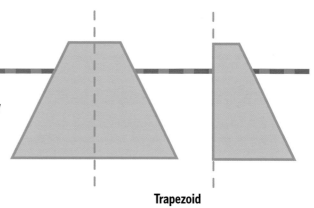

Trapezoid

Some figures have more than one line of symmetry. Some have none.

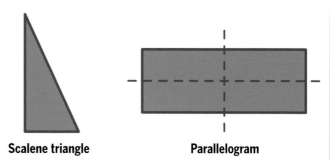

Scalene triangle   **Parallelogram**

If a figure has a line of symmetry, the two sides it divides are **congruent**.

Keywords
• symmetry
• line of symmetry
• congruent

Math

34

✴HELPSTER

PARTS OF SPEECH
Nouns: Common and Proper

Nouns are words that name people, places, things, or ideas.

▶ There are two main types of nouns: A **common noun** names a general person, place, or thing. A **proper noun** names a particular person, place, or thing.

Common Noun	Proper Noun	Common Noun	Proper Noun
girl	Keisha	dog	Rover
country	France	team	Los Angeles Lakers

Proper nouns always begin with a capital letter. Common nouns do not, unless they start a sentence.

I think <u>Keisha</u> loves <u>cake</u> more than anything.
<u>Cake</u> may be <u>Keisha's</u> favorite food.

Nouns often have the words *a*, *an*, or *the* before them. How do you know which one to use?

▶ *A* and *an* are **indefinite articles**. They are used with nouns that are not specific. Use *a* before nouns that begin with a consonant. Use *an* before nouns that begin with a vowel.

▶ *The* is a **definite article**. Use it for specific nouns.

> A and an are only used before singular nouns: <u>a</u> cat, <u>an</u> elephant.
>
> The can be used before singular or plural nouns: <u>the</u> cat, <u>the</u> cats.

Keywords
- nouns
- common noun
- proper noun
- indefinite articles
- definite article

✳HELPSTER

Perimeter

Perimeter is the distance around the outside of a figure.
You can find the perimeter by adding the lengths of the sides.
What is the perimeter of this figure? ⟶

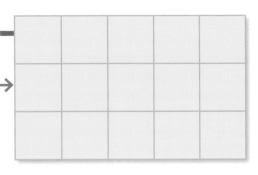

top	+	bottom	+	left	+	right		
5	+	5	+	3	+	3	=	16

The perimeter is 16 units.

You can also find the perimeter of some shapes using multiplication.

Rectangle	Square
4 in. [rectangle] 6 in.	8 cm [square]
Multiply the length by 2: $6 \times 2 = 12.$ Multiply the width by 2: $4 \times 2 = 8.$ Add the products: $12 + 8 = 20.$ The perimeter is 20 inches.	Multiply the length of a side by 4: $8 \times 4 = 32.$ The perimeter is 32 centimeters.

If the sides of a figure are equal, multiply the length of
one side by the total number of sides to find the perimeter.

Keywords
• perimeter

Math

Context Clues

Sometimes when you're reading, you'll come across a word you don't know. Maybe you can't read the word. Or maybe you don't know what it means.

Look at the words and pictures around the unknown word for help. These words and pictures are known as **context clues**.

Try these steps to use context clues:

▶ Look at the picture on the page. Maybe your word is shown in the picture. Try substituting something from the picture for the word in your sentence. See if it makes sense.

▶ See if the word is defined or described nearby.

Beverages, or drinks, are an important part of any birthday party.
(The context clue *drinks* defines the word *beverages*.)

▶ See if there are any examples that hint at the meaning of the word.
Examples are often introduced with the words *like*, *such as*, *include*, and *for example*.

Popular party beverages include water, juice, soda, and milk.
(The context clue gives examples that point to the meaning of beverages.)

Aha!

If using context clues doesn't help you figure out a word's meaning, you can always turn to your old friend the dictionary!

Keywords
• context clues

Area

Area is the number of **square units** needed to cover a figure.
What is the area of this figure? ⟶

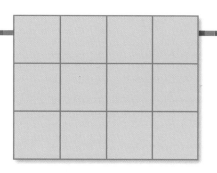

Count the square units in the figure.
There are 12 square units.
So the area is 12 square units.

You can also find area using multiplication.

Rectangle	Square
3 in. ▬▬▬ 10 in.	4 cm ▢
Multiply the length by the width: $10 \times 3 = 30$. The area is 30 square inches.	The length and width of a square are equal. Multiply the length of a side by itself: $4 \times 4 = 16$. The area is 16 square centimeters.

When you find the area, remember to label your answer in square units.

Keywords
• area
• square units

Homonyms: Homographs

Homonyms are words that are similar in some way. **Homographs** are a second type of homonym.

Homographs are words that are spelled alike but have different meanings. Sometimes homographs are also pronounced differently. Homographs are also known as multiple-meaning words. The word *homograph* comes from the Greek *homo*, meaning "same or similar," and *graph*, meaning "write."

Here are some examples. Do you know each word's different meanings?

Homograph	Meaning 1	Meaning 2
ball	I kicked the <u>ball</u> to my brother.	Cinderella dressed up for the <u>ball</u>.
bow*	He took a <u>bow</u>, bending gracefully.	She had a pink <u>bow</u> in her hair.
can	<u>Can</u> you help me?	This <u>can</u> of peas is old.
left	My friend Keisha writes with her <u>left</u> hand.	I accidentally <u>left</u> my homework behind.
light	This bag is heavy, not <u>light</u>!	Be sure to turn off the <u>light</u>.
wind*	The <u>wind</u> blew and made me cold.	You have to <u>wind</u> up that toy to make it go.
tear*	A <u>tear</u> came into my eye.	Be sure not to <u>tear</u> the paper.
nail	I need a hammer and <u>nail</u> to hang this picture.	The <u>nail</u> on my finger just broke.
dove*	The <u>dove</u> is a sign of peace.	He <u>dove</u> into the water.

* These homographs are pronounced differently.

Not sure which way to pronounce a homograph? Check a dictionary.

Keywords
- homonyms
- homographs

GEOMETRY
Solids

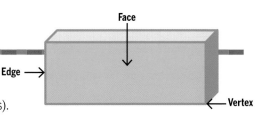

Face

Edge →

← Vertex

Solid figures are also called **three-dimensional figures**.
They are not flat.
A solid figure is made up of **faces**, **edges**, and **vertices** (corners).
Prisms have congruent shapes on their ends.

There are different kinds of solid figures.

Cube	**Cone**	**Cylinder**	**Sphere**	**Triangular prism**
6 faces, 12 edges, 8 vertices	1 flat face, 1 curved surface, 1 edge, 1 vertex	2 flat faces, 1 curved surface, 2 edges, 0 vertices	0 flat faces, 1 curved surface, 0 edges, 0 vertices	4 faces, 6 edges, 4 vertices

You can remember the kinds of solids by thinking of everyday objects. A cone looks like a party hat. A soup can is a cylinder. Can you think of others?

Keywords
- solid figures
- three-dimensional figures
- face
- edge
- vertices (vertex)
- prism
- cube
- cone
- cylinder
- sphere
- triangular prism

Math

*HELPSTER

37

Homonyms: Homophones

Homonyms are words that are similar in some way. **Homophones** are one type of homonym.

Homophones are words that sound the same but have different spellings and different meanings. The word *homophone* comes from the Greek words *homo*, meaning "same or similar," and *phone*, meaning "sound or voice."

Here are some examples.

Homophones	Example 1	Example 2
ad / add	That TV <u>ad</u> is really cool!	I can <u>add</u> 56 + 43.
be / bee	Could my sister <u>be</u> any meaner?	That <u>bee</u> almost stung me!
knew / new	He <u>knew</u> all the answers to the test.	The neighbors bought a <u>new</u> car.
pair / pear	Help! I can't find a matching <u>pair</u> of socks!	That <u>pear</u> looks ripe and ready to eat.
sea / see	From the boat, the <u>sea</u> looked calm.	Can you <u>see</u> that bird in the tree over there?
ate / eight	I already <u>ate</u> dinner.	Six plus two equals <u>eight</u>.
bail / bale	We had to <u>bail</u> all the water out of the boat.	The cows eat a <u>bale</u> of hay every day.
son / sun	He was the youngest <u>son</u> in the family.	I sure hope the <u>sun</u> shines tomorrow.
missed / mist	I can't believe I <u>missed</u> that basket!	I <u>mist</u> my hair with water to make it curly.

Not sure which spelling of a homophone to use? Look it up in a dictionary.

Keywords
- homonyms
- homophones

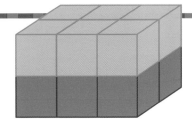

GEOMETRY
Volume

Volume is the measure of space inside a solid figure.
It is measured in **cubic units**.

Find the volume of this figure. ———→

Count the number of cubes in each layer.
Bottom layer: 6
Top layer: 6
$6 + 6 = 12$ cubic units

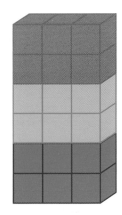

You can also find volume by multiplying.
Find the volume of this figure. ———→

Multiply the length by the width by the height.
$3 \times 1 \times 6 = 18$

The volume is 18 cubic inches.

When you find volume, remember to label your answer in cubic units.

Keywords
- volume
- cubic units

Math

✳HELPSTER

SPELLING AND VOCABULARY
Synonyms and Antonyms

Synonyms are words that have the same, or nearly the same, meaning.

Here are some pairs of synonyms.

happy / joyful	unhappy / sad
smart / intelligent	start / begin
sick / ill	end / finish
thin / skinny	big / large
house / home	car / automobile

Antonyms are words that have the opposite, or nearly the opposite, meaning.

Here are some pairs of antonyms.

happy / sad	love / hate
smart / dumb	fast / slow
sick / healthy	believe / doubt
thin / fat	big / small
pretty / ugly	nice / mean

To choose a synonym for a word, ask:
Which word has the same, or nearly the same, meaning?

To choose an antonym for a word, ask:
Which word has the opposite, or nearly the opposite, meaning?

Change the meaning of this sentence by replacing the underlined words with antonyms:

The <u>big</u> girl <u>loves</u> to ride in <u>fast</u> cars.

Keywords
• synonyms
• antonyms

8

Number Patterns

A **pattern** is a series of numbers or figures that follows a rule.

A dog has 4 legs. If you have 4 dogs, how many legs are there?

Number of Dogs	Number of Legs
1	4
2	8
3	12
4	?

Use a pattern to find out:

$$1 \times 4 = 4.$$
$$2 \times 4 = 8.$$
$$3 \times 4 = 12.$$

The rule for this pattern is: Number of dogs $\times$ 4 = number of legs.
If you have 4 dogs, there are 16 legs: $4 \times 4 = 16$.

Math

Patterns can follow addition rules, subtraction rules, multiplication rules, or division rules.

Keyword
• pattern

✳HELPSTER

Compound Words

A **compound word** is made up of two smaller words.

Take a look at these compound words.

after + noon = afternoon
basket + ball = basketball
door + bell = doorbell
any + where = anywhere
pop + corn = popcorn

To figure out the meaning of a compound word, first break it into its two smaller words. Think about the meaning of each smaller word. Then think about how those meanings could fit together. For instance, the verb *pop* means "to explode," and *corn* is "a type of grain." So *popcorn* is "a kind of grain that pops, or explodes."

Sometimes the meaning of a compound word is completely different from the meanings of its two smaller words. In that case, use context clues or a dictionary to find the word's meaning. Examples include *butterfly*, *dogwood*, *flapjack*, and *ladyfinger*.

Keywords
• compound word

*HELPSTER

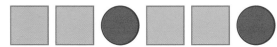

ALGEBRA
Geometric Patterns

A **geometric pattern** is a series of shapes that follows a rule.

What is the next shape in this pattern?

The pattern is: square, square, circle. So the next shape will be a square.

Here is another pattern. What is the next shape?

Triangle   **Quadrilateral**   **Pentagon**

Look at the number of sides. Each shape has one more side than the shape before it.
Triangle: 3 sides.   Quadrilateral: 4 sides.   Pentagon: 5 sides.

The next shape will have 6 sides: **hexagon**.

You can write the second example above as a number pattern: 3, 4, 5, 6.
The rule is: The number of sides + 1 = new polygon.

Keywords
- geometric pattern
- triangle
- quadrilateral
- pentagon
- hexagon

Math

✳HELPSTER

SPELLING AND VOCABULARY
Suffixes

Suffixes are groups of letters that can be added to the ends of words.
A suffix can change a word's meaning. It can also change its part of speech.

Here are some common suffixes.

Suffix	Meaning	Part of Speech	Words Containing the Suffix
-ed	in the past	verb	talked, looked, helped
-er	person who does	noun	dancer, painter, cleaner
-est	most or best	adjective	fastest, nicest, saddest
-ing	in the act of	verb / noun	singing, dancing, clapping
-ful	full of	adjective	wonderful, careful, cheerful
-tion	act or process of	noun	inspection, creation, protection
-sion	act or process of	noun	suspension, tension, comprehension
-able	able to have or do	adjective	comfortable, miserable, understandable
-ment	action or process	noun	movement, government

Sometimes, the spelling of a base word changes when you add a suffix.
- If a word ends in e, you usually drop the e before adding suffixes that begin
  with a vowel: <u>use + able = usable</u>.
- If a word ends with one consonant, you usually double that consonant before
  adding suffixes that begin with a vowel: <u>clap + ing = clapping, clap + er = clapper</u>.

Keyword
• suffixes

✖HELPSTER

6

Pictographs

A **pictograph** uses pictures or symbols to show **data**, or information. The **key** tells what each picture represents.

This pictograph shows how many hours Julia read each day.
How many hours does 1 book represent? How many hours did Julia read on Thursday?

Day	Number of Books
Monday	📖
Tuesday	📖 📖
Wednesday	📖
Thursday	📖 📖 📖
Friday	📖 📖

1 book = 2 hours.

Multiply the number of books by 2 to find out how many hours Julia read.

There are 2 whole books and $\frac{1}{2}$ book on Thursday.

$2 \times 2 = 4$ hours

$\frac{1}{2}$ book = $\frac{1}{2}$ of 2 hours = 1 hour

$4 + 1 = 5$

So Julia read for 5 hours on Thursday.

One symbol in a pictograph can stand for any number. If you had data with large numbers, you would use a larger number for the key.

Keywords
- pictograph
- data
- key

Math

41

HELPSTER

Prefixes

Prefixes are groups of letters that can be added to the beginnings of words. Prefixes have meanings of their own that they add to words. So a prefix changes a word's meaning.

Here are some common prefixes.

Prefix	Meaning	Words Containing the Prefix
un-	not, or the opposite of	unhappy, unusual, unfair
re-	again	retake, retell, redo
pre-	before	preview, preset
mis-	wrongly	mistake, misunderstood
dis-	not, or the opposite of	displease, disprove, dissatisfied
anti-	against or preventing	antidote, antiwar, antibiotic
fore-	before or in front of	forecast, forearm, foresee
bi-	two	bicycle, biweekly, bilevel

Keywords
• prefixes

Bar Graphs

A **bar graph** uses bars of different lengths to show data. You can make a bar graph from data in a **table**.

Favorite Activities of Third Graders

Activity	Number of Votes
Reading	9
Watching TV	5
Bike riding	8
Playing sports	12

← Table

Which activity is the most popular?

The label on the bottom of the graph shows the kind of activity.

The height of each bar shows how many students voted for each activity.

Playing sports got the most votes and has the tallest bar.

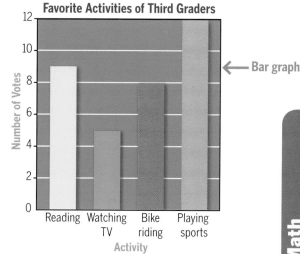

Favorite Activities of Third Graders

← Bar graph

If a bar falls between two numbers, it has the value halfway between the numbers. Nine students voted for reading, so the bar for reading falls between 8 and 10.

Keywords
• bar graph
• table

Math

*HELPSTER

42

SPELLING AND VOCABULARY
Root Words

Roots are word parts to which other word parts can be added. Knowing a word's root and what it means can be helpful. You can use the root to figure out the word's meaning.

Look at these examples.

Root	Definition	Words Using the Root
act	do or perform	action, react, actor
true	real or correct	untrue, truth, truthful
use	bring into action	useful, misuse, user

Many English roots come from Greek and Latin. Here are some common root words in English and their meanings.

Root	Meaning	Language It Comes from	Words Using the Root
graph	write	Greek	autograph, biography, graphic
tele	far away	Greek	television, telephone
phon	sound	Greek	phonics, vibraphone
vis	see	Latin	visit, invisible, visual
scrib, script	write	Latin	describe, prescription
dict	speak	Latin	diction, predict, dictator

Keyword
• roots

4

Venn Diagrams

A **Venn diagram** uses circles to compare related items. It shows what they have in common and what they don't.

Of the 30 students in Hannah's class, 14 have only a dog, 10 have only a cat, and 6 have both a dog and a cat. Here is a Venn diagram describing this information. ➞

The circle on the left shows all the people who have dogs. The circle on the right shows all the people who have cats. The overlapping part of the diagram shows the pet owners who have a cat and a dog.

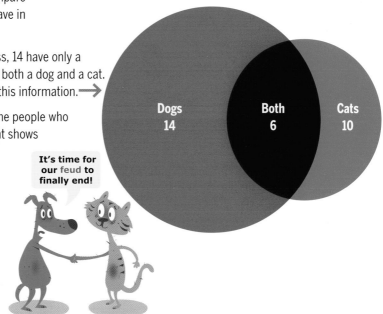

It's time for our **feud** to finally end!

You can also use a Venn diagram to sort numbers.

Math

Keywords
• Venn diagram

43

SPELLING AND VOCABULARY
Word Families

Word families are groups of words that contain the same sound. They often rhyme. What makes word families useful? Imagine that you know how to spell the word *cat*. Then you can spell *hat* and *mat*.

Here are some common word families.
Many have rhyming endings.

Word Family	Examples	Word Family	Examples
-ack	back, pack, black, stack	-ight	light, sight, bright, might, right
-ail	mail, pail, sail, wail, trail	-ing	sing, bring, wing, thing, sting
-ain	pain, stain, rain, drain	-ock	dock, stock, block, flock, knock
-ake	bake, cake, make, stake, brake	-ore	bore, sore, store, snore, shore
-ank	crank, flank, tank, thank, bank	-out	bout, shout, stout, trout
-eigh	weigh, eight, sleighs, neighbors	-uck	luck, buck, shuck, muck, truck
-ick	sick, thick, pick, flick, stick	-unk	plunk, hunk, skunk, junk, trunk

Some groups of words also share the same beginning sounds: street, straight, strand, struck. But that may not help with spelling other words: *stray, straight*.

Keywords
• word families

HELPSTER

3

Probability

Probability is the chance that something will happen. Suppose you spin this spinner.

An event that's **certain** will happen. It's certain you'll spin a letter that comes before E.
A **likely** event will probably happen, but might not. It's likely you'll spin a B.
An **unlikely** event might happen. It's unlikely you'll spin an A.
An **impossible** event can't happen. It's impossible to spin a D.

What are the **possible outcomes** if you spin both spinners?

A **tree diagram** shows the possible outcomes.

A	1	A1
	2	A2
	3	A3
B	1	B1
	2	B2
	3	B3
C	1	C1
	2	C2
	3	C3

There are 9 possible outcomes.

Probability can be written as a fraction.
The chance of spinning A and 2 is 1 in 9, or $\frac{1}{9}$.

Keywords
- probability
- certain
- likely
- unlikely
- impossible
- possible outcomes
- tree diagram

Math

SPELLING AND VOCABULARY
Consonants

In English, the **consonants** are *b, c, d, f, g, h, j, k, l, m, n, p, q, r, s, t, v, w, x, y,* and *z.* Each has its own sound.

Some consonants work together in combinations.

Consonant	Consonant Combinations	Examples
B	bl, br	blue, brave
C	ch, cl, ck, cr	chat, clap, pack, crab
D	dr	drag, drop
F	fl, fr	flat, frog
G	gl, gr	glad, grin
P	pl, pr	please, price
S	sh, sl, sm, st	ship, wash, slip, smart, start
T	th (makes two sounds), tr	that or thick, truck
W	wh	when, where

Certain consonant pairs or groups contain silent letters.

Consonant Pair or Group	Silent Letter	Examples
kn	the *k* is silent	know, knife
gh	either just the *h* is silent or both are silent	ghost, weigh
mb	the *b* is silent	lamb, comb
tch	the *t* is silent	catch, fetch, watch

Keyword
• consonants

2

Finding the Math

Read this **word problem**. How would you solve it?

Joe took pictures on vacation. He spent 3 days at the seashore.
He took 10 pictures the first day, 10 the next day, and 5 the last day.
How many pictures did Joe take in all?

1. Some problems have useless information that you don't
   need to solve the problem. Cross out useless information.
2. Underline the question.
3. Circle any **signal words**. These are words that tell you which
   operation to use: addition, subtraction, multiplication, or division.

Now the problem looks like this:

> Joe took pictures on vacation. ~~He spent 3 days at the seashore~~. He took
> 10 pictures the first day, 10 the next day, and 5 the last day. <u>How many
> pictures did Joe take in all?</u>

The signal words *in all* tell you to add up all the pictures: $10 + 10 + 5 = 25$.
Joe took 25 pictures in all.

Before you solve a word problem, always ask:
   What do I know?
   What do I need to find out?

Math

Keywords
- word problem
- signal words
- operation

SPELLING AND VOCABULARY
Vowels

In English, the **vowels** are a, e, i, o, and u.
Each vowel can make a long or short sound.

Vowel	Long Sound	Short Sound
a	cake	cat
e	Pete	pen
i	mile	mill
o	stole	sob
u	flute	hut

Words that end in a silent e usually have
a long vowel sound. Words with only
one vowel usually have a short vowel sound.

Some combinations of vowels are common.

Vowel Combinations	Examples
ai usually makes a long a sound	maid, paid, laid, raid, wait, bait, trait The <u>maid paid</u> the man for the <u>bait</u>.
ea usually makes a long e sound	eat, sea, treat, seat, bleat, beat, neat You can't <u>beat</u> a nice <u>treat</u> to <u>eat</u>.
ee usually makes the long e sound	see, sheep, sweet, beet, teeth, Are <u>sweet</u> <u>beets</u> bad for a <u>sheep's</u> <u>teeth</u>?
ie usually makes the long e sound	niece, piece, believe, brief, thief The <u>thief</u> stole a <u>piece</u> of cake.
ou usually makes an "ow" sound	shout, about, mouse, house, cloud, out Get that <u>mouse</u> <u>out</u> of the <u>house</u>!
oo can make two different sounds, a long one and a short one.	boot, shoot, food, soon, toot The <u>food</u> should be ready <u>soon</u>. book, shook, took I <u>shook</u> the <u>book</u> that <u>I took</u>.

The consonant y is sometimes used to make a long i sound. For example:
by, sly, fly, my, try, cry, why.

Keyword
• vowels

1

Solving

Make a **drawing** to help you solve a problem.

Kate made 15 cookies for her book club.
She wants to put 3 cookies in each bag.
How many bags can she fill?

Draw 15 cookies. Circle groups of 3.

How many groups of 3 are there?
There are 5 groups.
So Kate can fill 5 bags.

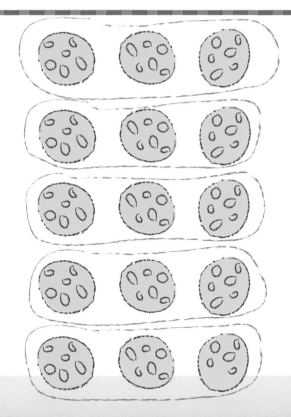

Language Arts **Keywords** (continued)

Solving (continued)

You can also use a **table** to help you solve problems.
Mr. Pine made a sign-up sheet for after-school volunteer work.
Which day has the most volunteers?

Monday	Tuesday	Wednesday
Rosemary	Christine	Robin
Mark	Michael	Donna
Scott	David	Keri
Michelle	April	Gene
Pat		Jan
Lee		

Day	Tally	Number
Monday	|||||		6
Tuesday	||||	4
Wednesday	|||||	5

Monday has the most volunteers.

Sometimes you can use more than one strategy to help you solve a problem.

Keywords
• drawing
• table

Math

47

Language Arts **Keywords**

WORD PROBLEMS
Checking Your Work

Make sure you check your work after you solve a word problem.

Lisa's doll is 2 feet tall. Gretchen's doll is 20 inches tall. Whose doll is taller?

Steve said that Lisa's doll is taller.
An answer is **reasonable** if it makes sense.
Is Steve's answer reasonable?

You know that 1 foot = 12 inches.

So 2 feet = 2 × 12 = 24 inches.

24 > 20, so Steve's answer is reasonable.

Check Steve's work by working backward:

24 ÷ 2 = 12 and 12 inches = 1 foot, so Lisa's doll is 2 feet tall, and that's taller than 20 inches.

Math

Language Arts Contents (continued)

Checking Your Work (continued)

Now solve this problem:

> Carl has 8 jazz CDs. Victoria has 3 jazz CDs.
> How many more jazz CDs does Carl have than Victoria?

You can solve the problem like this: $8 - 3 = 5$.

Carl has 5 more jazz CDs than Victoria.

> You can check your answer by using the **inverse operation**.
> Addition is the inverse operation of subtraction.
> $5 + 3 = 8$, so the answer is correct.

Check division problems by using its inverse operation, multiplication.

Keywords
• reasonable
• inverse operation

✶HELPSTER

Language Arts Contents

ISBN-13: 978-1-60214-000-4

Play Bac Publishing USA, Inc.
225 Varick Street
New York, NY 10014-4381

Printed in China

Distributed by
Black Dog & Leventhal Publishers, Inc.
151 West 19th Street
New York, NY 10011

First printing, January 2007

Play Bac Publishing wishes to thank all the teachers, mothers, and children
who have helped develop the books in the Helpster series.

SPECIAL THANKS to: Anne Burrus, Catherine Rupf, Sue Macy, Gramercy Books Service,
Steve Tomecek, Susan Buckley, Sunita Apte, Justine Henning, Joan L. Giurdanella,
Joe and Denise Kiernan, and the great team at the Bill SMITH STUDIO.

All the books in the Play Bac series have been tested by families and teachers
and edited and proofread by professionals in the field.

Please send your comments to:
Play Bac Publishing
225 Varick Street
New York, NY 10014-4381

Thanks!